Children and Anger, you can do it!

....

A guide to becoming better parents,
and not passing on your anger to your children.

•

EMILY KENDALL

....

Copyright © 2021 Emily Kendall

All rights reserved.

CONTENTS

Introduction	5
Chapter 1: WHAT IS ANGER, REALLY?	9
Chapter 2: WHY YOU LOSE YOUR MIND	27
Chapter 3: ANGER AFFECTS PEOPLE DIFFERENTLY	43
Chapter 4: ANGER TODAY	59
Chapter 5: PUSHING BUTTONS	73
Chapter 6: TROUBLE WITH TANTRUMS	91
Chapter 7: HOW TO TAME YOUR BEAST	105
Chapter 8: COMMUNICATION IS KEY	121
Conclusion	133

Introduction

CHAOS, MADNESS, FRUSTRATION, CHILDREN

Do you ever feel like your children must have been somehow influenced by the god of chaos? It's almost as though they don't have the capacity to understand the word 'peaceful.'

Well, you know what? You're not alone. And they probably don't have the capacity.

You know that feeling; your blood feels like it may be boiling. Your heart is beating in your throat, and a cold sweat breaks on your forehead. You're late for work; your seven-year-old is dawdling, and the two-year-old is running around without a diaper at the kind of speed that seems impossible. You wonder how such tiny legs can move so fast.

Just as you think that you've caught the little bugger, they smash into your freshly pressed shirt with sticky hands. The older one knocks over a bowl of cereal, and their outfit is ruined. You freeze…

That is it; your children freeze with you. Again, fear clearly sprawled over their faces, and it felt as though they might be holding their breaths. This time, you actually notice it. It stops you in your tracks. Are they… afraid of you?

Your partner rushes forward and grabs the little one with one arm and tugs at the other with their other arm. You're left standing alone in the corridor. The anger was seemingly forgotten; the only feeling that is left is the crushing pain of the realization that your own children may be afraid of you.

And your partner knows it. The guilt is unbearable. If something similar has happened to you recently, or if you've recently yelled at your child and suddenly realized that their tears sting deeper than whatever it was that caused the outburst... then this book is for you.

Your situation may be different, though; you may simply have realized that you blow your lid off too often. Your patience may be a little thin, or you may be having trouble communicating with your children or your partner.

Did you know that angry parenting tends to be passed down through generations? You might have noticed your own angry parenting recently or some time ago. Surely, it will get you thinking about your own childhood. Were you a victim of angry parenting as well?

What a word, victim. It sounds so harsh that it's difficult to swallow. But yes, you might have been a victim, and your own children may be as well. Nothing good comes from angry parenting. And I know it hurts to hear it, but it's damaging. The very last thing that we want is to damage the people that we love more than anything else in the world, our own flesh and blood.

Therefore, we need to look within ourselves; we need to learn about what the issues are. What our triggers are, and what we can do to prevent these outbursts. And most importantly, what we can do to prevent our children from being classified as victims. It took years in order to gather all the knowledge that I have today, don't feel bad for not knowing something. Nobody knows anything until they reach out and learn!

Furthermore, you know what? It is not just us; even celebrities like Brad Pitt have had issues dealing with anger and parenting. Angelina Jolie cited that his anger management issues mixed with parenting were one of the main reasons she filed for divorce, as it was affecting her kids (Renfro, 2016).

I'm not going to lie; it is not easy. In order to change, you need to face your demons—all of them. You need to critically analyze yourself, your parenting, your own parents, and more. But it's worth it. My firstborn was the hardest; I was clueless. I was drawn into the thought that yelling was a part of parenting.

I was convinced that the way I was raised was probably the right way. I didn't realize that it was completely off track until my own heart broke at the sight of my crying daughter.

The journey was long and frustrating, but I made it. And you can too. The end result? Peaceful parenting, guilt-free living, and mutual respect. If you can imagine it for a moment, you can realize that the journey is worth the effort.

You are worthy of a good life, and your children are too. And it all starts with you. You are capable of so much more than you think, and control and healing are just within your reach.

Grab the opportunity for self-growth; grab the opportunity for a better tomorrow for your children and even their children.

If we do this right, then perhaps our children will not have to recover from their childhoods. And within a generation or two, we might be able to finally change the world.

It all begins with you.

Chapter 1:
WHAT IS ANGER, REALLY?

Do you have an anger problem? If you're reading this, then the chances are that your answer is yes.

In this chapter, you will discover the real meaning of your anger and how it affects you and your children.

DEFINING THE WORD 'ANGER'

Having different emotions makes you human. Some emotions are more intense than others, and anger is definitely one of them. It's an emotion that is typically displayed when something has not gone the way you had planned or when someone has wronged you in some way (Ohwovoriole, 2021).

Although the emotion can be described as intense, it's not always a bad thing. Anger is often thought of as negative, and it surely is. However, it also helps you express your feelings and can be described as a way to focus on solving the causes of your anger.

It's also thought of as an automatic response to many negative situations (Psychology of Anger, 2015). It has been mentioned that anger can be thought of not as a primary emotion but rather as a secondary emotion. Why? Because you're never just angry.

Anger mostly goes hand in hand with some kind of mental or physical anguish. As humans, we're inclined to want to blame something or someone for our pain. In many cases, we might even blame ourselves, and therefore, the anger is targeted at someone (or even something).

Sometimes, we might get angry because of our own thoughts. For example, your two-year-old is constantly crying and throwing things around. You instantly think that this is an ill-behaved child who wants to taunt you. These thoughts anger you, and so it begins. However, two-yearolds are not trying to taunt you at all. They simply have overwhelming emotions that they don't know how to deal with.

But we'll discuss this in more detail later on. A simple example, really, but it goes to show that the thoughts you have that trigger your actual anger are not always accurate at all. Your assumptions can be your downfall when it comes to this intense emotion, and many people act before they have all their facts together.

Your emotions can also be difficult to keep to yourself, even when you do realize that you need to calm down. Feelings of anger can easily be given away by your body language, such as the expressions on your face and how you move your hands. This can negatively affect your relationship with people around you.

Everyone gets angry, and it's completely normal. However, it becomes a problem when you cannot control the anger inside of you and when the anger becomes too frequent.

Anger also has other physical signs that run deeper than your body language.

There are signs that you might have an anger problem that can help you spot your issue before it becomes an untamable problem.

Here are the most common signs, you might not be experiencing all of them, but if you are experiencing quite a few of them, that signals a problem.

- You have recurrent outbursts that you can't seem to control. It creeps up with slow intensity, and before you can realize it, you've been consumed by your anger. During these outbursts, all rationality can seem to fly out the window. These outbursts are usually followed by even more intense feelings of shame, guilt, and grief over your actions.

- You're easily and often irritated and/or annoyed. The

smallest thing can set you off. Your partner may have a certain habit that has never bothered you before but suddenly drives you insane. Your son might be singing a school tune over and over again, or you might even be feeling this way towards yourself.

- You're the one who starts the arguments and/or the bickering. Being easily annoyed/irritated can lead to starting unnecessary arguments that provoke your partner or other people around you.

- The people who live with or work with you seem to be on edge when you're around. You can literally notice that they almost seem to retract within themselves when you're around. It's an unpleasant feeling, realizing that people seem to be afraid of your reactions. There's a difference between being respected and being feared.

- You seem to have trouble expressing how you feel. Of course, you want to tell people what is bothering you, but it always comes out the wrong way or leads to unnecessary shouting and unpleasant situations.

- When you do try to express how you feel, and it turns out negatively, or when people do speak out against you, you tend to resort more to verbal or even physical violence. This does not mean that you're physically abusive (although it can), but you might be prone to hitting your fists on the table or even throwing and/or breaking things. When it comes to verbal violence, you sometimes find it hard to put your emotions into words and therefore begin using cuss words or even verbally abusing the people around you.

- You feel anger too often throughout your day. It might be a low-intensity type of anger that you feel in your chest that you can contain, or it might even be full-blown anger.

There are also physical signs/symptoms of anger that most people experience. When your anger is intense, and you might have a problem, these symptoms may be much more apparent, to the point where it may cause physical health issues.

I once knew a man who very clearly had anger management issues, and one day his fit of rage shot his heart into a state of atrial fibrillation. Atrial fibrillation is a condition where the heart beats abnormally irregularly and usually very fast. This is typically more common in men than in women, and it's a real risk.

The man's heart was in a state of fibrillation for a long time before the normal heart rhythm could be corrected via surgery. Other symptoms of atrial fibrillation may include severe fatigue, dizziness, and shortness of breath.

Atrial fibrillation is mostly short-lived, but persistent atrial fibrillation, as with the case above, can last for months. It's more common in older men; however, the man mentioned above was around the age of 50, which is not typically thought of as 'old.'

Granted, he had a history of heart problems, but the risk remains, and the amount of stress you put your body under during a fit of rage is not healthy.

Here are some of the physical signs/symptoms of intense anger.

- Muscle tension from anger can be excruciating, to the point where it can even cause a fierce headache or other muscle spasms.
- Your heart rate will increase; some people do not notice this, and others feel it very clearly.
- Have you ever felt your face and/or ears warm to the touch? It's basically flushing, but not the good kind.
- During your bouts of anger, you may also notice that you clench your jaws or fists to the point where it becomes painful.
- A tight feeling in your chest may also result.

A good tip would be to slow down during your bouts of anger and to focus on your breathing and the physical signs and/or symptoms. Once you slow down to focus on yourself, you'll likely find the time to calm down as well.

WHY ANGRY PARENTING IS BAD

It's probably the most well-known reason out there, angry parenting upsets your children, and it also upsets you. Children look up to us as their protectors; when we give in to our anger, we go against that. You may not always feel that way, but you are your child's comfort. It's a fundamental shock when the source of their protection and comfort turns around and becomes the source of their fear.

It may sound a little tough, but in reality, it's true. Children can easily start fearing you when you are prone to outbursts that may include shouting and the likes. As a parent, saying this is heartbreaking for the simple reason that no parent wants to be feared by their children. We want to be looked up to, loved, and respected. There is a fine line between respect and fear, and I would say that it comes down to your parenting style.

There are four main types of parenting, according to Diana Baumrind in the 1960s, namely Authoritative parenting, Authoritarian parenting, Permissive parenting, and Neglectful parenting. Authoritative parenting is probably the style of parenting that most of us aim for. There are clear rules, and the parenting is firm yet warm, supportive, and loving. These parents have reasonable expectations of their children and are typically quite involved with their lives.

The problem comes in with Authoritarian parenting; some people who experience issues with anger management and angry parenting tend to lean more towards that. Authoritarian parenting is much more intense when it comes to rules and discipline. To the point where it can border on abuse (whether it be physical or mental). Parents who indulge in this style of parenting often expect blind obedience and have high expectations for their children that are non-negotiable (Li, 2018). They are also not as involved with the lives of their children as the above-mentioned.

Permissive parenting is probably way on the other side of the line with few to no rules. These parents are typically very warm towards their children and have trouble with using the word 'No.' And neglectful parenting is, as the name states, neglectful. Parents often have their own mental health issues that lead to being uninvolved and indifferent behavior.

Now that you know a little more about some common parenting styles, which one do you think suits you? Remember, you may not fall into one category alone but rather into a combination of two or even three categories.

When it comes to angry parenting and often Authoritarian parenting, the anger only fuels the negative situations that have already developed. As they often say, "you can't fight fire with fire."

Angry parenting also causes deeper issues in your children than simply upsetting them; it can cause mental, cognitive, and emotional issues as well. It's not only the fact that it affects them directly when it's directed at them, but anger management issues and other negative emotions are easily spotted by children as well.

I've often heard people describing children as sponges, and I have spent a good amount of time thinking about that. They absorb everything around them, from your smallest habits to your fits of rage. Even something as seemingly insignificant as nail-biting can be picked up by your child. And despite the stigma, men are just as likely to bite their nails as women are. It's typically a sign of anxiety and stress rather than anything else.

Children who grow up in stressful situations are more prone to anxiety and, therefore, such a habit if they constantly witness their parents doing it. While we might think the opposite, certain research does show that the mental health of the fathers does have more of an effect than the mental health of the mothers (Gonzales, 2019).

As a father, you might feel as though you do not play as big a role as mothers do because of the picture that the world has painted. But in all reality, fathers are equally as important as mothers when it comes to parenting. Not only does the responsibility of raising said children also fall on your shoulders, but the responsibility for their mental health also falls upon you.

Even the emotional states of absent parents affect their children, whether it be mother or father. Again, children are like sponges. Something that we don't like to think about is the fact that children often turn to blame themselves. They don't understand your frustration and your anger, and therefore, they take it upon themselves. That causes even further damage.

All things considered, I do understand how true anger can blur one's judgment, and I understand how it may cause overreaction. It can cause the showcasing of a version of you that you don't often let the world see. It makes it difficult to think before you speak.

Anger can make you into a completely different person, depending on what angered you and how far you've been pushed. Most people have this breaking point, but you need to take a breath and consider the people around you, especially your children.

HOW ANGER AND HOSTILITY AFFECT YOUR KIDS

There are signs that a child is living in a stressful situation and that the child may have 'angry' parents (Australia, 2020).

Of course, these signs could signal other issues, but they are common amongst these children. This is especially common for children who have anger and frustration directed toward them.

- They have trouble concentrating, and their academic ability may be affected.
- They may have trouble with social interactions.
- They may withdraw within themselves and become quieter.
- They may become the opposite of the above and actually become louder and 'rude'; thus, their behavior in different situations may become what is considered 'bad.'
- They may display signs of aggression towards other people, especially their peers, leading to the conclusion that they, themselves, have now developed anger issues.
- They may have trouble with either sleeping too much or too little.
- They may have trouble interpreting their emotions. While most children have this issue when they are

younger, it can become a problem as they get older.
- They have had trouble with self-control in different aspects of life.
- Their problem-solving skills may be affected.
- They will probably live in constant fear of the wrath of whoever has the anger management issues in their lives.
- It may also lead to your child becoming a victim of bullying in school, as they may not have the right understanding of boundaries, and their self-esteem may be very low.

These negative effects can be life-long. Regardless of our state of mind and how angry and/or frustrated we get, we still love our children. There is not one parent reading this today that harbors true ill wishes towards their children. We want to see them flourish; we want to see them happy and content.

The fact that you're reading this book says as much; you want to be better. That in itself is commendable. It's heartbreaking

to truly realize the effects that our frustrations can have on our children; it's enough to push a person to tears.

Therefore, we must be better, and we must do it before it is too late.

They say that the forming years are up until the age of seven.

I believe that with love and compassion, any child can be taught and changed. This means that you should not feel bad if your children are already older. It's never too late!

WHEN THEY'RE ALL GROWN UP

With that being said, if the anger issues are not resolved, the negative effects on your children can last into adulthood. So, I suppose the term should be, "it's almost never too late."

There are many ways that your anger can affect their adult lives. Their mental health may suffer severely, depending on how dire the situation is. And that may also lead to trouble with maintaining healthy relationships, jobs, and more.

Adults who stem from houses where anger and anger outbursts were a regular occurrence have been described as either one or the other. What I mean is that they may either develop these issues themselves or withdraw so much within themselves that they become very susceptible to abusive relationships.

There is no way of telling which effect will be more prominent in a child; another common occurrence is that they may become the 'quiet' type who seems to be withdrawn and abused, rather than abusive, yet have trouble with bottling up their anger. This kind of anger can be bottled up for months or years, and when it finally explodes, it can become a very unpleasant situation and very distressing for the people close by.

When it comes to other mental-health-related topics, anxiety and low self-esteem are the most common long-term effects.

However, there have been reports of children suffering from Post-traumatic Stress Disorder or PTSD. This is an illness that can severely alter their quality of life as the thoughts and feelings that go with it are often all-consuming (Mayo Clinic, 2018).

There are so many other mental-health-related issues that may occur that it can be frightening to think about. But we need to think about these things so that the severity of the situation sinks in. Your anger management issues do not make you a bad person or a bad parent. But, if you don't handle it correctly, it may cause the kind of damage that you would not wish on anyone, much less your own children.

THINK BEFORE YOU SPEAK

It goes without saying, words hurt. In fact, words may hurt more than physical pain. Yes, I acknowledge that physical pain may cause psychological scars, and that is a topic on its own. But your words may linger just as long.

For children, words cause a lot of pain. Especially when the 'mean' words come from someone that they love and trust. It's a huge shock for a child when the person that is supposed to protect them turns out to be the one who hurts them.

When you think about it from their perspective, it becomes clear that you need to really think about what you say before you speak. Impulsive speaking raises the risk of saying things that may seriously damage your relationship with your child.

I remember a young girl from my youth; she was no older than twenty years old when we met. After getting to know the girl, I realized that her seriously damaged self-esteem also stemmed from childhood. In fact, her father was the one who told her that she would not get a date to prom if she did not do something about her weight.

It stayed with her for life, and that's how serious your words are. They can make or break your children. In this sense, it's not only about what you say to them in anger; it's also what you say in general! You may not even realize that your words are hurtful.

Anger can easily damage your relationship and/or bond with your child to the point where communication is less frequent or open, and your child may even begin to fear you. As you know, this is the worst feeling that a parent can experience. But it's just as bad for the children.

These cracks that may result from angry parenting/outbursts of anger will need to be fixed. If there is nothing done in order to fix these cracks, the outcome will be negative in more ways than one.

Think about how you feel about your own parents. Some people have fond memories; others do not. In fact, I know people who carry true resentment for their parents. I can't even imagine my children resenting me one day. But the fact is, if we don't work on ourselves and fix the cracks that may have already happened, they may very well feel that way about us in the future. Not to mention the lack of social skills and issues with healthy relationships in their own lives, as we've discussed.

Here are some things that you can do in order to work on your bond with your child or to strengthen the bond. We don't like to think about it, but even now, some damage may have already been done.

- Frequently tell them that they are loved, but don't just tell them; show them.
- Make time for bonding experiences!
- Play with the younger ones, and try to show genuine interest in their hobbies and/or interests. Especially for older children. It will mean the world for them to have you involved. I suppose one must still be careful not to

become a helicopter parent. Teenagers may not enjoy this! But even if you don't always involve yourself in what they enjoy doing, talk about it. Ask them questions about their music, even if it's awful in your opinion.

- Even when the whole family can't have a meal together for whatever reason, try to make a point of having meals with your child.
- Listen to your children. We don't always understand the importance of this. We need to listen to them and take in what they say. If they're not interested in ballet, or sports, listen to them. Silly example, but it will mean a lot to your child if you show them that you care about how they feel.
- Therapy and/or counseling is always a good idea. Both individually and together.

Now that you understand exactly what anger is and how it may affect your children throughout childhood and adulthood let's look at why it happens.

Chapter 2:
WHY YOU LOSE YOUR MIND

When you get all fired up, it can be tough to push it back and lock it away... Next, we will cover why you get angry, how upbringing affects the way you parent, and why your anger isn't your fault, but the actions you make are.

It's not necessarily about locking your anger or any other feelings away. In fact, I would say that this is not effective at all. Instead of locking them away, you need to deal with them. In order to do that, you need to know why.

WHY ANGER MIGHT CREEP UP

The first and probably most common reason why people get so angry is because of bottled-up emotions. It may even be a series of smaller annoyances or other small things that build up and build up until you get to a point where it cannot be kept inside anymore..

It could be the way your partner keeps the television volume too high when you need to focus on your emails or the way your boss smirks when you sigh. It could be more substantial emotional issues that you keep to yourself. There are many things it could be, and the first step to solving the problem is to recognize what the main issues are and deal with them instead of sweeping them aside. For smaller annoyances that build up over time, it might be helpful to address these issues with the people involved. It's good to let them know how you feel; in fact, communication is crucial for any relationship with anyone. In chapter 10, we'll discuss why and how in more detail.

The second most common reason for anger would-be triggers; in this case, you might not keep your feelings to yourself but rather clearly show your anger at whatever your trigger may be, big or small. We'll also take a deeper look into triggers a little later on.

I suppose the third most common reason is probably the one that we all know too well. Exhaustion. Exhaustion is a funny thing; it can make you behave very differently than you normally would, and it can also severely cloud your judg- ment. Pair that with true anger, and you have a disaster on your hands.

When we're not sleeping enough, frustration can take hold. You're tired, and everyone around you seems to not be thinking about you or what you need. It feels frustrating, and you feel the anger creeping up. In fact, you might be frus- trated with one thing, and then another may come up, and that's where you blow your top. This can especially be the case. You may be tired because of your long hours and other work-related things, but it comes out when your three-year- old starts throwing a tantrum. Similarly, you may be frus- trated because your newborn has not been sleeping well, which is related to exhaustion, and then blow your top at work. In this sense, it all connects once again to bottled-up emotions.

PARENTING TAKES ITS TOLL

There's nothing quite as frustrating as a child that stares you right in the eyes as they do the thing that they were told not to do. It's no wonder that anger may overflow at this point, especially when they might be damaging something that you value or endangering themselves.

That little girl looks you right in the eye as she knocks over your grandmother's vase or jumps off a high table. Especially if there have been many attempts at reprimanding them leading up to the case. I know a lady who broke down and cried one day because her toddler was eating her makeup constantly. She would buy a new lipstick and find it eaten the next day.

Sure, there should be simple solutions to problems such as this. Put it where the kid can't get to it? But in reality, that's not always as easy as it may seem. Unless you literally lock your things away, trust me, they'll get to it. These little buggers can climb, after all.

When it comes to more dangerous things, such as your chronic medication, or anything that may possibly harm them, I really do recommend that you lock it away so that there is no chance that your little one can get to it.

When they're this little, it's as if their sense of safety hasn't kicked in yet. That's why it's important to teach them about safety with certain things and to ensure that they are reprimanded and that they know about consequences for trespassing where they should not.

Where does anger come in? When you've tried all that you can, and they still end up going against your word. This is understandably frustrating and leads to understandable anger. However, the emphasis lies on how you handle the situation once more.

It can sometimes feel like a never-ending cycle; you reprimand them, they do it again, you reprimand them, and they throw a tantrum. I don't know if any of you know what I mean when I refer to the 'screech,' but this is probably the most angering and frustrating thing that I have ever experi- enced. Sure, children cry when their upset. I'm a reasonable person; even if I don't understand why not being able to chew on my laptop upsets them, I understand that it may be upsetting and that the result may be a few tears.

However, the 'screech' is a sound that reasonably terrifies parents. It starts with a few tears. The high-pitched screech that comes next is probably the most horrid-sounding thing that I have ever heard. It's enough to hurt the ears; why it occurs, I cannot say. But I know that it's enough to drive me through the roof.

In all reality, if you've never experienced bad behavior such as the above mentioned, I can safely say that your turn might be just around the corner. So many people want to blame children or their upbringing for bad behavior, and in a small sense, it does play a role. But in the bigger scheme of things, some bad behavior and some tantrums are a part of growing up.

They go through so many phases, and their bodies, minds, and emotions are ever-changing. It's no wonder that they, too, get frustrated from time to time. Educating older chil- dren on how to deal with their emotions is very important; however, when it comes to smaller children, it's not that easy.

Even if you try explaining certain things to them, they may still not understand, and that could lead to even more frustration or bouts of the 'screech.' That's why it's important to know how to handle your own emotions and anger, in order to better support the little one before you.

CONTROLLING YOUR ANGER AS A PARENT IS NOT EASY

That being said, even knowing all these things doesn't always make it easier. Especially when you think about how so many books and articles tell you that you need to focus on yourself and that you need some alone time.

Can I just say, of course, we need alone time, we're human beings. But the problem is, we have little rascals that we're responsible for, and some people do not have the finances for paid help or have the strong support systems that others have. In a perfect world, the grandparents would help out with the kids every second weekend or so. The nanny would step in once a week so that you and your partner could enjoy some time together. But you know what? We don't all have that, and that's why existing anger management issues can still be toxic and even more difficult to handle.

In truth, I've seen cases where it can be difficult to handle even when parents get their little moments alone. That being said, having a few minutes to yourself will definitely help. Even if you just sit in your car for a few minutes to calm down. So, one can't just blame that, but it definitely plays a role. Even when you have someone to help you every now and again, it's still frustrating when you can't use the bath- room on your own on most days or you have a tiny foot in your face when you're trying to sleep.

If you take anything from this, take the fact that it is difficult, and that's okay. Many different things make controlling your anger as a parent difficult to do. You never truly know what another person is experiencing in their own life.

HOW YOUR UPBRINGING AFFECTS YOUR PARENTING

When you think back to your childhood, are you daydreaming in fondness over the kind-hearted mother with the red lipstick and her perfume that hugs you when you cry? About your father playing catch with you and the smell of his cologne when he shows you the affection that a child needs? Do you think about good food, laughter, and bedtime stories?

Or, do you cringe at the angry voices, possible abuse, and anxious feelings that your childhood evoked? You see, the way you were brought up actually does play a big role in the way you will respond to parenting. You may not notice it at first, but with time, when you really look at yourself and think, you will.

People respond differently to their childhoods; some people are spitting images of their parents, whether that be a good or a bad thing. While the trauma might last the same, some people will make a point of trying to be better than their parents were. That's a pretty great mindset to have; wanting to be better for your children is definitely a good thing. However, some people take it too far.

It also reminds me of a man I once knew who came from an incredibly traumatic childhood. Untreated mental health illnesses ran throughout the family. While having a mental health illness is nothing to be ashamed of, it can indeed be treated to ensure a happy and healthy life. However, when it's left untreated or even undiagnosed, there may be grave consequences.

Pete realized this as he became older; he was diagnosed with mental health illnesses and received treatment. He also did his fair share of research, and this made him realize that his mother and many of his siblings (he had six) probably suffered from similar conditions.

He made it his life's mission to ensure that his children did not suffer the way he did. However, he took it too far, and the results that he hoped for turned out to be the opposite. Instead of trying to find a reasonable balance between repri- manding them and affection, he opted for basically no conse- quences at all. Of course, his children, being children, took advantage of this, and their behavior became unbearable.

This is an example of what could happen, but the opposite could also happen just as easily. Parents may be too strict because they were raised by uninvolved parents. Parents may be prone to anger and violent outbursts because of their childhood. It all comes down to the proper treatment and processing of your experiences.

While Pete may have received treatment for his mental health, his childhood trauma was never truly addressed because many people (especially older generations) do not want to speak ill of their parents, regardless of what they've done. It's almost as though they are ashamed or as though the respect that they have for their parents triumphs over their own need for care and treatment.

I don't condone blaming other people for your behavior at all, but if you wish to truly work through your childhood trauma, you need to find the source. Mental health plays a big role, of course. People who suffer from depression will often tell you that there is no real reason for them being depressed; they simply have a chemical imbalance in their brains.

With that being said, childhood trauma may also lead to depression and other issues. It's important to seek out the help you need and deserve. A professional will be able to help you find the root of your feelings, regardless of what that root may be. If it turns out that your childhood is the root, they can help you work through it and process it.

Therefore, the first step to being successful at parenting is processing your own trauma and working through your own issues in order to be better for your children.

People who have unresolved issues that stem from their own childhoods may display the following behaviors, among others.

- They often find it difficult to bond with their partners and their children. This can lead to uninvolved parenting, trouble between spouses, and more. Bonding with your family is crucial. These are the people that you love the most, that love you the most.
- They may be prone to passive-aggressive behavior; this means that they do not directly or openly share their feelings, mostly their negative feelings. They may, instead, express them more indirectly. It has been said that there is a visible difference between what they do and what they say (Hall-Flavin, n.d.).
- They may also be prone to emotional and/or physical neglect.

HAVING THESE ISSUES ARE NOT YOUR FAULT, BUT YOUR ACTIONS ARE

By now, I suppose you understand why it's important to break the cycle of generational trauma from your upbring- ing. Transgenerational trauma is like a cycle; it doesn't end with one person. It continues through different generations (Dixon, 2021b).

In reality, it can affect any of us. Anything can be carried over through generations, and it's not always bad. However, transgenerational trauma refers to the negative. It has been said that families with a history of severe abuse are more commonly affected.

The fact is, whatever the trauma that you carry might be, it can and has to stop with you. If you're reading this and thinking about how relatable it might be, that's a good first step. Realizing that there are things that need to be addressed and worked through.

You want your children to have a better life than you did; you want them to have healthy relationships and to know how to work through anger management if it is present. Therefore, you need to start the work right away. Your trauma is not your fault, and your problems are not your fault. But what you do here and now, and how you act, that is up to you.

You have the power to break the cycle. You are worthy of a happy and healthy life, and so are your kids! There is no perfect time to get help; the time is now. There will never be a perfect moment; you need to make your own perfect moment.

COMMON MISCONCEPTIONS ABOUT SEEKING OUT THE HELP YOU NEED

There is a lot of stigma surrounding mental health, especially when it comes to men. Men are just as likely to suffer from mental health conditions as women. In fact, studies have shown that men are even more likely than women, and the risk of suicide can be even higher (Campbell, 2019).

That's another topic that might be sensitive to cover, suicide. With generational trauma, mental illness can often be a result. Untreated mental illness accompanied by unresolved trauma may lead to a higher risk of suicide. The world has been painting men as these strong, independent providers. People often don't take their mental health as seriously as they should, and the results are nothing short of terrifying.

Any person with mental health conditions needs the proper help and care, but men are less likely to reach out and admit that they have a problem. The stigma that surrounds this issue is a leading cause.

It's almost as though they see it as a sign of weakness. The problem with this mindset is that it not only negatively affects you but also negatively affects the people around you.

Untreated mental health conditions can become dangerous to other people, both in men and women.

As a father, you don't need to be strong all the time. You're still a person, and even though we would like to be able to work through all of our issues and problems alone, we can't. And that's okay! There are trained professionals for a reason! If we could handle everything on our own, all the time, there would be no professionals who dedicate their lives to helping us.

If you have trouble with anger management, past traumas, depression, or anything else, get the help you need! You know what? It takes a strong man to admit that he has a problem and to actively do something about it!

Professionals will be able to help you manage your anger, and stress in more ways than you ever thought possible. Of course, there are self-help books out there, like this one, that will try their best to help you as much as possible. For some, that is enough. But realizing the extent of your problem is important. Deeper emotional traumas require more exten- sive treatment. It helps to read about tips and to take the advice of people who may have been where you are, but in some cases, you might need specific medications.

Another problem that we face is the stigma surrounding medication. So many people are ashamed of needing to take the medication in order to live a happy and healthy life. The fact is, I don't see how it's something to be ashamed of. Should diabetics be ashamed of their medication? Should cancer patients be ashamed of their medication? Whatever the case may be, your mental health conditions are chronic conditions that require treatment, just like any physical condition.

Instead of focusing on the medication itself, focus on the results that they bring! Yes, you may need medication to function normally, but you're functioning normally! You're living a good life that might have been much harder without it.

Own your conditions and be proud of who you are and the fact that you are bettering yourself. Not only for your chil- dren or other family members but for yourself and your own quality of life as well.

BE GENTLE AND UNDERSTANDING

Just like we want our loved ones to be gentle and understanding towards us, we need to be gentle and understanding towards them. Living with someone who has certain conditions is not always easy.

Even if your only problem is the fact that you get frustrated with your children after a hard day at work and you have trouble controlling your anger, put yourself in their shoes. I have found that this is a great way to help you control your anger. Stop and think about how the other involved person is feeling.

You are a loving parent; that's why you're here today. Don't be afraid to show that! Everybody gets angry, and it affects most people differently. Let's have a look at how anger can affect different people.

Chapter 3:
ANGER AFFECTS PEOPLE DIFFERENTLY

Anger affects people differently, and there are many things that make this statement true. Two great examples are your gender and personality type. There is evidence that these things can make differences ranging from small to quite significant. It's also really great to know more about your own personality type. This helps you prepare for certain situations more effectively.

MEN VS. WOMEN AND ANGRY PARENTING

While men are more likely to become aggressive, women get just as angry, just as frequently as men. They simply have a different way of showing it. When it comes to parenting, simply not being physically aggressive is not enough. Aggressive language is just as damaging to children, if not more.

Some might say that it stems from power, the reason why men are more prone to angry parenting, that is. I read an article by Virginia Pelley called "Why Good Men Are Bad To Their Families." I thought the title was a little offensive, but the content of the article did make sense.

In this article, the scene is set by describing a man who was a generally pleasant man. His colleagues seemed to like him, he easily made friends, and he was a generally pleasant person to be around. However, that changed when he got home. The scene describes what we've been discussing a lot over the last few pages, but it's a little different. See, the man in question is a pleasant man, which can be the case. But when frustra- tion builds up in a way that we've been discussing, you prob- ably won't be so pleasant at work anymore.

What made sense to me was how they described that since your home is your "safe place," it's easier to "let your hair down" and be "meaner" (Pelley, 2018). That means that while it's not too bad to keep yourself in place everywhere else, it's harder to do so at home. In my opinion, this is probably the case with both men and women. But the article made it more about male power in the home. It stated that when you're the one in charge, it's easier to voice your anger. Even in this mod- ern world, it's still common for men to assume the role of the head of the house. It's not a bad thing, but I suppose it does make it easier to be less responsible for your actions.

In my opinion, this all led to the bad reputation that fathers have for angry parenting. While it can be true, mothers are, as we've discussed, just as prone to anger. In fact, there is even a specific term for it; mom rage. Apparently, it's a rela- tively new concept. But if you're a man who has ever had a pregnant wife, you'll know it's true. Now, that is a little bit of a joke. Real mom rage is said to be much worse than your typical frustrated mother.

Fathers have bad reputations for angry parenting because men have bad reputations for anger and abuse. It's only in recent years that any kind of movement has been made to create awareness around the fact that men can be victims of abuse as well. It's actually much more common than you would think. But it hasn't been spoken of as much because men are often ashamed about the abuse that they suffer from, which can lead to transgenerational trauma, which furthers our toxic cycle. If you or someone you care about are victims of abuse, you need to speak out and get the help that you need.

When you look even deeper into the past, it may also come down to toxic masculinity. If you have not heard the term before, it means that society pressures men to act a certain way. Be manly, don't cry, and don't be a 'weakling.' This also plays into why many men don't seek help for mental health concerns and why men don't speak out against their abusers.

It's especially a problem with earlier generations. Young boys were victims of toxic masculinity, and their fathers might have been especially hard on them. Boys don't feel it like girls do, right? They need to be tough, right? Wrong. A little boy needs just as much affection and care as a little girl. When you're raised by parents who may have come from a different time, before this was even known, your upbringing may be traumatic without you realizing it.

Whether you or any other person realizes that your trauma might stem from your childhood or not, it has an effect on your parenting. If we want our boys to become strong men who are not afraid of their emotions and who are gentle yet firm, we need to break free from the influences of our parents and follow our hearts.

I've met fathers who would cry when they felt they needed to be extra firm with their sons. One particular man comes to mind. He was taught that his boy needs to be beaten and brought up a certain way. Let's call him Joe for the purpose of keeping his identity private.

Joe was the kind of man who looked, well, like you would expect an older man who was brought up in a strict house to look like. But, he had a gentle heart, and he loved his son more than anything. I was told that Joe often wept with sorrow when he needed to reprimand his son. Or rather, when he felt he needed to. There is nothing wrong with reprimanding children, but how you do it makes all the difference.

I remember thinking to myself that if this man felt in his heart that the way he was raised, the way he supposedly needs to raise his son, is wrong, then why? It can become almost like a form of indoctrination. Parents believe that they are doing the right thing, even when it feels wrong.

In all actuality, your little boy is going to be a naughty little thing, just like any other child. You need to be firm, of course, but you are allowed to hold your little boy tight and to let him know that he is loved and that he is allowed to feel and show his emotions too.

Now, none of this means that girls are raised without any difficult times, not at all. Traditionally, women were raised to be homemakers. Luckily, this was stopped in its tracks way before there was ever any attention brought to toxic masculinity in all its forms. However, there are still certain pressures and injustices that women face today.

That's what makes parenting difficult, two people coming together who may or may not have faced their own trau- matic experiences, trying to be better for their little ones. It's no easy task, but it's possible.

Women are typically presented as being less angry than men, but that is simply not the case. Women have their own difficulties that they need to face. The difference is that women (in general) are less likely to become physically aggressive, or so it has been believed for years. Some studies would still support this claim, and I suppose while there is some truth to it, it's not set in stone.

I was trying to understand what the cause for this may be. I researched and read for days. I read about hormones and other things that play a role. But I came across something that actually had me shook. I read that most women are less likely to become physically aggressive or show their anger in general to a certain extent because of their fear of retaliation. Can this be because of the reputation that men have for anger? I believe that it might.

Many of the things that have been mentioned above directly relate to angry parenting. If men have bad reputations when it comes to anger, of course, their reputations as angry parents would not be much better. I suppose a reputation is a reputation for a reason. Surely, there is some truth in it. But it's not the rule, and I believe that the growing popular saying "not all men" would definitely apply here as well.

Now, when it comes to your personality type, there have been studies that show that different personality types react differently. This supposedly presents in both men and women. Some are more dominant than others, but the prin- ciple remains the same.

HOW DIFFERENT PERSONALITY TYPES HANDLE ANGER

In the year 1917, two American women began researching personalities. Isabel Briggs Myers and her mother, Katherine Cook Briggs, decided to embark on this journey because of a simple realization; Katherine noticed that her new son-in-law had very different personality traits than other members of the family.

The entire story began with curiosity and led to a world of discovery. A man named Carl Jung had a similar theory, but his theory was more complex. They studied his theory and his work and furthered their own.

Eventually, after years of research and modifications, it came down to the Myers-Briggs Personality Type Indicator that we know today. Finding out what your personality type is, is actually quite fun! It helps you to learn a lot about yourself. But before we go into how you can do that, let's take a look at the different personality types and how they deal with anger specifically.

I read an article by Kendra Cherry that I thought was very informative; it explained the system in an easy-to-under- stand way. The article was published in July 2021 on the Verywellmind website. There are sixteen personality types, according to Myers and Briggs. They place emphasis on the fact that these personality types are not a reason to look for faults within yourself but rather to look for better ways to understand yourself.

Extraversion (E) - Introversion (I) was actually a part of Jung's original work. Extraverts, spelled differently than you normally would, are said to be "outward-turning," while Introverts are placed as "inward-turning" (Cherry, 2021).

Extraverts are the kinds of people who enjoy spending time with other people, tend to talk more than others, and have no problem with taking the lead or being the center of attention. In comparison, Introverts prefer spending time on their own and are said to look for deeper connections and interactions with the few people that they do enjoy being around.

Sensing (S) - Intuition (N) is said to be a vital scale; Myers and Briggs imply that you lean either to the one or the other. Those who are more prone to sensing are said to be the kinds of people who are keen to learn and gather physical experiences. They typically pay a lot of attention to their senses in order to accomplish that. Those more prone to intuition typically enjoy pondering on possibilities and future adventures and often focus more on things such as patterns and possible impressions.

Thinking (T) - Feeling (F) is about how people make decisions. The thinking kind would probably be more comfortable with making decisions based on stone-cold facts after they've spent a good amount of time considering the pros and the cons. On the other hand, the feeling kind is more likely to make emotional decisions.

Judging (J) - Perceiving (P) relates to how you deal with more than just your own thoughts and decisions. Those who are more prone to judging have rules that are set in stone, and they prefer structure and routine over chaos, whereas the perceiving kind are more likely to be open to change; they're also much more adaptable in situations involving change.

Now that you know what the letters mean, it's easier to understand the different combinations. Let's look at the sixteen known combinations/personality types. I will give a short explanation of each type, and I encourage you to look them up for further study!

1. ISTJ (Introversion, Sensing, Thinking, Judging), also known as "the inspector," this personality type is known for being more introverted and logical. They're often said to be keen on routine and organization. They're also quite loyal.

2. ISTP (Introversion, Sensing, Thinking, Perceiving), also known as "the crafter," is also more prone to introverted behavior, but they are said to enjoy adventure and physical experiences.

3. ISFJ (Introversion, Sensing, Feeling, Judging) is also known as "the protector" this personality type is probably the

kind of person you'd like to have around. They're not overly loud, and they tend to have a warm personality. They're also pretty responsible.

4. ISFP (Introversion, Sensing, Feeling, Perceiving) is also known as "the artist" this personality type is an easy-to-work-with type of person. They don't go looking for trouble, and they're also described as friendly and creative.

5. INFJ (Introversion, Intuition, Feeling, Judging), also known as "the advocate," is probably the rarest personality type. It has been said that they often feel misplaced or misjudged. They're an interesting mixture of emotion and logic, and their personality often contradicts themselves.

6. INFP (Introversion, Intuition, Feeling, Perceiving) is also known as "the mediator" they're creative, yet also a little introverted, and they're said to have high standards that they stick to. However, they are also difficult for people to understand.

7. INTJ (Introversion, Intuition, Thinking, Judging) is also referred to as "the architect" this personality type analyzes everything, and they tend to lean more towards logical thinking.

8. INTP (Introversion, Intuition, Thinking, Perceiving), also known as "the thinker," tend to be very introverted; they

spend a lot of time thinking about, well, everything. They often overthink as a result.

9. ESTP (Extraversion, Sensing, Thinking, Perceiving) is also known as "the persuader" this personality type is sometimes referred to as the "drama kings and queens" of the personality types. They're very energetic and extroverted as well.

10. ESTJ (Extraversion, Sensing, Thinking, Judging), also known as "the director," is probably what you would call a "goody-two-shoes." That's a good thing, as rules mean a lot to them. They're also known for being very assertive.

11. ESFP (Extraversion, Sensing, Feeling, Perceiving) is also known as "the performer" this personality type is probably exactly what you think about first when you hear the word extrovert. Spontaneous and loud!

12. ESFJ (Extraversion, Sensing, Feeling, Judging), also known as "the caregiver," is also extroverted, but they tend to also be warm and comforting. They enjoy encouraging other people and seeing others succeed.

13. ENFP (Extraversion, Intuition, Feeling, Perceiving) is also referred to as "the champion" this personality type is very independent and innovative. They sometimes tend to be disorganized, though.

14. ENFJ (Extraversion, Intuition, Feeling, Judging), also

known as "the giver," is typically described as very persuasive yet empathetic and encouraging.

15.   ENTP (Extraversion, Intuition, Thinking, Perceiving) is also known as "the debater" this personality type is described as smart and creative. They are solution- driven, and they obviously enjoy a good debate. However, some think they are a little more on the "know-it-all" side.

16.   ENTJ (Extraversion, Intuition, Thinning, Judging), also known as "the commander," is as the nickname would suggest. A true leader who is not afraid to make difficult decisions.

HOW EACH PERSONALITY TYPE DEALS WITH ANGER

1.   ISTJ (the protector) is said to be very quiet about their anger. They keep it to themselves yet make comments about the people that they're angry with that will definitely hint at the fact that they're upset.

2.   ISTP (the crafter) personality types tend to fight their anger with other things; they may be drinking heavily or over-exercising. They also don't seem to enjoy engaging with the specific person/people that they are angry with.

3.   ISFJ (the protector) personality types are said to be

passive-aggressive as well, but they tend to pretend as though nothing is upsetting them. Of course, this leads to bottled-up emotions, which can quickly escalate, as you know by now.

4.   ISFP (the artist) can definitely hold a grudge for a long time; they may walk out of your life and never return. The anger can boil in them for years. At the moment, they usually clearly show their anger.

5.   INFJ (the advocate) personality types seem to be the kind of people who rarely get really angered. They may simply avoid you until they've calmed down. On the other hand, when they do get angry, it can get pretty nasty pretty quickly.

6.   INFP (the mediator) personality types would rather walk away and think about the situation that angered them. They like to analyze whether they may be wrong or whether they may be overreacting.

7.   INTJ (the architect) would probably not be too bothered about you when you anger them. They will simply decide for themselves that you were simply amateurish to begin with.

8.   INTP (the thinker) is similar to ISFP (the artist), but they will eventually snap and resort to breaking people down.

9.   ESTP (the persuader) is more physical about their anger, they may not physically abuse anyone (although they could), but they're the kind who may toss plates at you.

10.   ESTJ (the director) get annoyed pretty quickly, they often want things their way, and they're angered by people who fail to stick to that.

11.   ESFP (the performer) personality types overreact pretty easily, but they're also the first to apologize and calm things down.

12.   ESFJ (the caregiver) personality types are easy to forgive, but they're not the type to forget.

13.   ENFP (the champion) really takes the time to see the situation from the other person's perspective by putting themselves in their shoes. However, they are a little on the egotistical side and may shame the other person for not doing something the way they would have done it.

14.   ENFJ (the giver) personality types are likely to show their anger; however, they may either step away to think about the situation or verbally attack the other person.

15.   ENTP (the debater) often hits below the belt with their insults. They are prone to fits of rage, but they may antagonize the person to whom their anger is directed for quite a while.

16.   ENTJ (the commander) will carefully think about how they can get back at the person that they are upset with. They may plan this for quite a while.

As mentioned before, these are simply short descriptions that will give you a better idea of what they mean. I recom- mend checking out the website "16personalities.com" in order to help you find exactly what your personality type is and what that means.

Of the sixteen personality types that have been mentioned, four of them are the most likely to get very angry, and they show that anger or act on it. In fact, the ISFP (the artist) per- sonality type is said to be the most likely of all. Here are the others.

ENFJ (the giver)

ESFP (the performer)

ISTP (the crafter)

Knowing your personality type may help you to resolve some of your issues in the long run. There is a lot more that can be learned from your personality type and about yourself than you know.

Do yourself the favor of researching the above-mentioned!

Chapter 4:
ANGER TODAY

Technology is growing every day, and the more it spreads, the harder it is to cut out of your life. Your family's electronics could be contributing to the anger brewing in you...

HOW TECHNOLOGY AFFECTS YOUR ANGER

In this modern world, it can be difficult to pull ourselves or our families away from cellphones, laptops, televisions, or any other kind of technology. The funny thing is that we often fight our children on the fact, but we're often just as guilty as they are.

I remember sitting in the park one day, simply people-watching and enjoying the sunny day. There was a little girl with bright blue eyes and a yellow dress. I assumed she was around the age of three. She was playing in the park, and her mother was on her cellphone.

Many stories came rushing to my mind about how easily children are kidnapped these days while their parents are otherwise occupied. At that very moment, the little girl ran to her mother and started tugging on her baby blue sundress.

I could see that the child obviously wanted to show her mother something, and the mom simply ignored her. After a few more minutes of tugging, she burst out in a fit of rage and yelled at the little girl to go and play because she was busy.

I was completely taken aback. It raised a whole other problem. I realized that I was guilty of that, too, getting upset over kids bothering me when I was on my phone or laptop. I can see why it would annoy a parent, you're clearly busy with something, and they don't seem to understand.

It's good to look at the situation from their point of view. They want to spend time with you, and they want to be around you. But we only see a child who isn't taking no for an answer when we sometimes don't even take a moment to tell them no.

We often get upset when our kids spend too much time on their phones or whatever the case may be. We know that it's bad for them, and so we encourage them to play outside or to spend time with their friends in person. But do we realize that it's just as bad for us?

When we're angry with them for being online so much, do we stop to think that we're the same? And that children often do as they see? Again, children are like sponges. And not checking ourselves with the same kinds of rules that we check them with may lead to what they call "distracted parenting," which basically sums up the opening paragraph of this chapter.

The fact is, it all really comes down to multi-tasking. Trying to focus on a million other things while your kids are 'nag- ging' you is difficult. It often makes one very irritable and easily driven over the edge. When you're working, it can be difficult to focus on your kids and on your work. This is especially true for parents who may work from home or parents who often take work home. Now, when you've spent the whole day working, and they continue to need your attention in your "free time," that's when parents also often snap.

Technology is also the center of so many arguments, not only between parents and children but between adults as well. I could go into detail about all the things that could happen online but should not, but let's assume that the parents in question are faithful to each other. Other argu- ments that may arise between partners are that the one or the other does not spend enough time with the children or them.

Not to mention that your online life makes it easier to make negative comments about other people without much of the consequences that you would have had, had it been in person. It fuels anger because of this; it's easier to stay angry with someone or to even act out on your anger, even if it's not in person.

This is just as much of a risk for our kids. There's nothing quite as nasty as an angry child/teenager. Internet bullying has become a popular thing in this day and age. And it can even be dangerous. When kids are upset with a classmate, they don't walk over to them during recess anymore; they post something horrible about them on the internet for the whole world to see.

Of course, the risk of suicide by internet bullying has gone through the roof in recent years, as it becomes easier and easier to get away with internet bullying. It's no different with adults. You'd think adults would have some form of restraint, but I've seen some very nasty comments being made by adults towards others.

Whether you're the victim of internet bullying, or the one doing the bullying, this form of technology negatively affects you and your anger management issues. The saddest part of all of this is that you can get so sucked in by your online life that you forget about your real life.

At the beginning of this chapter, I mentioned a woman who got angry when her little girl distracted her from her phone. The dangers that were mentioned are very real. If you have not read up about it, I suggest that you do. There are count- less tragic stories of children being snatched up right from under their parent's noses while they were busy on their phones. At parks, in grocery stores, practically anywhere.

Some years ago, there was a group of people who made a video to demonstrate how easily it can happen. Forgive me, but I do not recall who they were. In this video, I saw a man pretend to lure children with candy and then snatch them up and run. The parents mostly did not even notice until later. Sometimes, so much time went by that the guy had to walk up to the parent and tell them what just happened. My insides turned as I thought about what could have happened had that man been a real kidnapper. From that day on, I vowed to be more vigilant.

Dangers aside, the other risk is the fact that we don't spend enough quality time with our families anymore. We spend our days glued to our laptops for work, and then we spend our evenings glued to our phones for entertainment. When do we make time for the children? The little girl at the begin- ning of the chapter simply wanted to show her mother something; she wanted her mother to be involved in her playing and to be with her.

Time goes by so quickly that the risk of missing too much of their lives is very real. It's not only that when we get angry with our kids for wanting our attention, we also hurt their feelings. Specific trauma can actually develop because of this. Emotional neglect is probably a much more serious case, but it has dire consequences for the children that may last for the rest of their lives.

Kids are emotional beings; actually, humans are emotional beings. An emotional connection and affection are essential for children and for us to thrive. I know that you love your kids, and you do not want them to ever feel emotionally neglected. That's why you're here. It's something to think about the next time you get annoyed with them when you're online. Again, thinking of it from their perspective might just be what helps you to calm down.

Children who feel emotionally neglected are also more prone to "acting out." They may realize that they are simply not getting our attention in the normal way, and therefore they may resort to bad behavior. The very first time that I heard this, I thought it was nonsense, to be honest.

I didn't really believe the whole "naughty kids want attention, and even bad attention is attention" thing. Until I decided to dig a little deeper, and I realized that it was actu- ally true. Especially when parents are incredibly busy, too busy for their kids, they will find other ways to get your attention.

Now, you may think that this only happens with smaller children, but teenagers show the same behavior as well. In fact, many "badly behaved" teenagers started acting out when they were little in order to get the attention of their parents, found that it worked, and then kept on doing that.

Preventing this from happening is simpler than you might

think. Good old-fashioned quality time and a little bit of firm discipline. I suppose it's different when you already have a teenager who is very set in their ways. You know, as much emphasis as we place on our mental health, we also need to consider theirs. A teenager such as this may definitely require professional help. And that's okay too, as long as you're actively taking the steps towards helping them.

On that note, it's important to watch out for signs of other mental health conditions in your children as well. It's definitely worth looking up if you have not already done so. In order for them to thrive, they need to be physically and mentally healthy.

Your Kids and Technology

Now, we know that too much screen time is bad for our children and for us; we even know a few of the reasons why. But let's take a deeper look at why screen time is bad for chil- dren. I found reading up about this to be helpful because kids love to ask 'why,' and answering them with a simple "because I said so" is not good enough; in fact, that has proven to actu- ally be damaging in other ways. Therefore, it's good to be armed with the correct responses. It's also good to know exactly why in order for us to understand the full extent of the situation.

There is really no limit to what can be put on the internet. We have all these cool functions now, such as Youtube kids and other parental locks and restrictions. However, you'd be surprised at what still gets past these restrictions. I've seen some pretty disturbing "kids shows" around. It's not simply about being disturbing or not being appropriate; some of these seemingly harmless shows actually promote bad behavior.

It's a good idea to be vigilant and to really go through what you're letting your kids watch. Don't just assume that it's child-friendly because it says so. There have even been instances where children had gotten up to dangerous things, or things harmful to others, because of what they saw on television.

Not to mention that too much screen time takes away from reading, playing, and learning. If kids don't explore the mud, their ability to jump around or read enough, the risk of them having developmental issues is a real possibility. One good example of this is an inability to focus on anything else when the television is on, or they have a tablet or other form of technology playing. This negatively affects their concentra- tion in the long run as well.

Speaking of the long run, too much screen time may even affect their ability to properly socialize. Even teenagers are at risk of isolating themselves from other kids their age or even their families because of the online lives that they have created for themselves. That obviously negatively affects the rest of their lives as adults as well, since social interaction is crucial for almost everything when you're an adult, including your career.

Smaller children may become isolated by spending most of their time in front of the screen. I've seen little ones at restaurants who sit in front of the televisions that some restaurants have in the kiddie play area instead of playing with the others. And they stay there for their entire visit. That's a simple example; however, I am sure that you under- stand what I mean.

Too much screen time may also have an impact on their mental health in other, more serious situations. There have been reports of children who have seriously started battling with things such as depression, a short memory span, insom- nia, excessive crying, and more. It may even cause an unhealthy dependency on technology, regardless of what form it may be in; dependency on anything that is bad for your health is inevitably a bad thing. I think it's safe to say that in all reality, too much screen time is not good for them, and you know what? A lot of those mentioned above are exactly the same for adults.

DITCHING THE ELECTRONICS AT HOME

Now that we know how bad too much technology can be for all parties involved, let's look at the benefits of limiting the use of online platforms and other technology.

- Spending more time together is the first benefit that comes to mind. Spending time with your loved ones is essential for you, your partner, and your children. It leads to deeper connections, trust, and understanding. You want your kids to be able to trust you and talk to you, right? Spending more time with them, without your phone, will definitely help in this regard. It's also good for your mental health to spend time with people that you love and who love you.

- Children who feel safe loved, and heard are less likely to act out. By spending more quality time with them, you can create an encouraging environment that will benefit them in the long run. You're also less likely to be stressed and annoyed when you know that your phone is gone for a certain period of time and that this means that the time is indeed free time.

- Let's face it, we all know that feeling of pure exhaustion. You crave your bed all day and wish for blissful sleep to comfort you, only to be glued to your phone for hours before finally going to sleep. Older kids likely know this feeling too. As you now understand, sleep is crucial. When you set rules in place for both you and your children, you will be getting more sleep, and that will benefit both your physical and mental health.

- At first, kids may be upset over their loss of screen time, and tantrums might be a little rough. However, once the new routine has set in, you will definitely realize a drop in how frequently they throw tantrums. Children often voice their need for screen time very loudly, and by taking it away and setting a new routine, you will definitely see improvement.

- Once you've successfully limited your online time, you'll notice that you may get more things done than you thought you could in a day. Your children will also likely spend more time on creative play and homework!

- And finally, the one you've been waiting for, reducing your online time will lead to less stress and less angry parenting! When you take everything into consideration, it's easy to realize how exactly this is possible. Less screen time leads to fewer of those angry outbursts that occur when kids want your attention and fewer arguments over their screen time.

At this point, you're probably sold on the fact that less screen time/technology use is better! But you're probably thinking 'how'? To some of you, it may even sound somewhat impossible. But, let me tell you, it's not. And it's actually easier than you might think.

HOW TO LIMIT THE USE OF ELECTRONICS

When we were younger, technology was absolutely a thing. We're not that old. However, we still have a lot more freedom and a lot more time outside than kids have today. When I say freedom, I literally mean freedom. It's as though cell phones and other more modern technologies have taken humanity as their prisoners. For all the reasons that have been mentioned so far, we need to break these chains and take back our lives.

- The simplest way to start is to have dinner together as a family, without cell phones. It's not a big change, and like any addiction, it's good to start small. You may be frowning at the word 'addiction,' but I find it to be a very accurate description of the situation. We are, indeed, addicted to our technology. But never fear, that's why we're here! To break away.

- Your second step is to set a good example for the children. Kids tend to look at us and ask, "if you can, why can't I?" This is not the time to reply with "because I'm a grown-up" this is the time to show them that you know how bad it is for yourself as well, and therefore, you are also making the change.

- Thirdly, you'll want to regulate the amount of time they spend with their cell phones/laptops/tablets, or whatever the case may be, in general. This can come a little later than the above two steps. Say about a week in, but don't let it be a surprise. Talk to the family and let them know that changes are going to gradually start coming. For example, you can have a "no television during the week" rule. Or a "no cell phones during the week" rule for younger kids. When it comes to teens, I don't think that taking their phones away for the whole week is the best idea; that's a recipe for rebellion. However, you can still have them put their phones away, perhaps in a box, while doing homework, eating, and when it's lights out. In this case, you can also put your phone away when you're working, unless you need your phone for work, in which case you can explain that to them. You can also put your phone away before bedtime. It has been said that putting your phone away an hour or two before bedtime will help you sleep better anyway!

- During the first few weeks, you will need to prepare yourself for constant battles. Yes, it will be tough. But it will absolutely be worth it in the long run. Ensure that you are calm when this does happen.

- Create fun activities that kids will enjoy doing that do not involve technology. Outside play and/or board games are a great idea!

- You might even create a room in your house where no electronics are allowed at all, such as the dining room or the living room. It could be a fun place for family activities and meals.

It may sound like a lot of work now, but you won't regret it. Once the whole family is used to the new way, you'll see that everyone will be better off, and they won't even miss it anymore!

Chapter 5:
PUSHING BUTTONS

A nother simple anecdote might be helpful in explaining. My friend Lisa for example, was having a tough week at work, and she often worked overtime. She was exhausted and irritable, and then her 7-year-old son Brennan decided to throw a fit about going to soccer prac- tice one afternoon.

At that moment, it all became too much, and she just exploded on him in a fit of rage, yelling at him until he started crying. And Her husband came in and dealt with Brennan so that she could go calm down. This is a perfect example of something that happens to parents all the time, especially if they have anger issues.

Her trigger in this situation was likely her son not wanting to go to soccer practice after she had gone through an intense amount of effort to get him there, despite her busy schedule. I suppose this would be a trigger for most parents. Tantrums are triggers!

There are other triggers that one should be aware of as well, and we'll discuss how to recognize them and what to do about them, and what to do about being triggered by tantrums in the pages to come.

TRIGGERS AND SET-OFFS

As we know by now, children and their behavior can be a big trigger for most of us, especially those who may be prone to angry parenting and/or anger management issues. Triggers are more than simple bad behavior, though; they can be the smallest things or the biggest things. They can come from your children, your partner, colleagues, and family or friends. You might not believe it, but things that have nothing to do with people may also be triggers for anger. The type of triggers that I want to discuss in more detail would be emotional triggers.

What we classify as an emotional trigger could be anything from a single object to a word. Our own memories can also be emotional triggers. These memories can, in turn, also be triggered by our surroundings. However, some people have these memories for no practical reason. That means that they jump out at you, out of nowhere.

Emotional triggers that are often referred to as trauma triggers usually stem from deeper trauma, and if you notice that you have real emotional triggers that disrupt your life, seeking professional help is a good option. It has been said that emotional triggers do not only cause emotional symp- toms but physical symptoms as well that may mimic anxiety.

The problem with emotional triggers is that they may also

negatively affect your parenting skills. Especially if those triggers stem from your own childhood trauma, this may make it difficult to cope with day-to-day parenting.

Anger triggers are another emotional trigger that makes parenting difficult. These are the ones that are difficult to contain. It may seem similar to having a problem with anger management, but it's not quite the same. Anger management issues can be triggered by many different things; they don't specifically relate to one specific thing or event, as we've previously discussed.

However, true anger triggers also stem from trauma. I suppose it depends on the person. Trauma affects people differently. Just like with anger management issues, the victim is often left in a state of feeling helpless and power- less. As though controlling themselves is difficult.

It's good to identify the triggers throughout your life. Unfortunately, most emotional triggers do require professional intervention. However, there are a few things that you can do alongside your treatment that may help.

When you're trying to identify your triggers, you should pay attention to when your symptoms begin. Whether they're symptoms of anger and/or anxiety, but specifically anger, in this case.

Force yourself to take a moment and recognize what the situation around you is at the moment.

- Are there other people around?

- If so, was it something they did or said?

- Was it something that did not relate to people at all?

- Was it perhaps a certain smell?

- Was it a feeling that resulted because of a situation?

It has also been suggested to try and identify your triggers outside of the moment. For example, taking some time to be by yourself in order to quietly reflect on your past and where symptoms began. Others say that this is easier with the help of a mental health professional, as they may offer helpful advice in recognizing where the root of the issue stems from.

HOW TO AVOID YOUR TRIGGERS

Once you've realized that you do indeed have triggers, and you've recognized one or more, it may become easier to deal with. It's not always possible to avoid your triggers, especially if one of your triggers may be a specific person, which is a very real possibility. You may carry a grudge against someone for something they did or said, and that grudge may lead to deep resentment. In that case, working through your own emotions internally is the only true way to go about it.

If your triggers relate to the behavior of other people, it's always good to communicate this with them, regardless of who they are. Talking about how you feel and what bothers you isn't always easy, especially in certain toxic work environments. It sounds utterly ridiculous, but some workplaces discourage it completely. I feel like that's so toxic that it can become triggering in itself.

If your triggers relate to family members or friends, it's usually easier to express your feelings. In any case, it's essential to set your boundaries and to communicate them with the people around you. Whatever your boundaries may be, you are allowed to voice them and to have them respected.

If there is no way that you can communicate your feelings or be heard, it's always a good idea to simply walk away. For example, some people are very triggered by others who enjoy a drink. This can be because of past trauma stemming from someone who might have had a drinking problem in their lives or perhaps from battling with their own drinking problem.

Other people enjoying a drink is not necessarily a bad thing, and you can't exactly tell everyone at the function to stop drinking. Depending on the severity of your situation, you can walk away if you need to.

This method helps for triggers that are not related to people as well; if a certain smell triggers you, avoid it. Whenever you can avoid a trigger, it is good to do so. And when it cannot be avoided at all, it may be a good idea to think about why that is and what can be done about it.

WHEN KIDS PUSH YOUR BUTTONS

Earlier, we discussed how little kids have this naughty little habit where they will look you straight in the eye and then do the thing that they were told not to do. It's probably one of the most frustrating parts of parenthood, especially when it comes to older children. After a good amount of research, most of us understand that little ones go through a phase and that it's a part of their development. We're therefore firm yet understanding.

However, dealing with older kids and teenagers who do the same is a whole different story. The older they get, the better they seem to get at pushing our buttons. It's like fine art that every child learns at one point or another. And getting a parent to flip their lid over it is almost like a right of passage.

The term "pushing buttons" can be explained in different ways. In the most obvious way, it's explained as losing your temper because of things your kids or other people do that they know to annoy you. However, it can also be explained differently, and the child in question may be pushing buttons in a way that runs deeper than a simple annoyance.

As we know, most little ones push our buttons for various reasons, including pushing boundaries. Older kids are differ- ent. They enjoy pushing our buttons because it might amuse them to see us lose our cool (although this is rare), they may need attention, or they may even want something to go their way, and they think that by manipulating us, it will work out in the end.

As for deeper related issues, some people, including one of your children, may especially be prone to pushing your buttons without it really being their fault. It could all simply come down to you. An example that I read in an article was about a mom who has two daughters, and she was more likely to get upset and annoyed with the older one for the same behavior that the little one showed.

Upon deeper inspection, it was found that the mother was also the eldest sibling and her parents were not very involved, and when they were, they scolded her for the behavior of the little ones. So she needed to assume respon- sibility for them, in a way. Therefore, in her mind, the older one had to be way more mature than the little one.

This is obviously a problematic way of thinking. Firstly, they're your kids, and while older siblings can always help out, they really should not be the ones who are mainly responsible for the little ones.

Secondly, the older child must have felt a world of emotions at realizing that the little one was getting away with a lot of things that she, herself, would not be able to get away with. In the end, these things cause emotional issues that may again lead to trauma that is brought over to the next genera- tion and the next.

With all this being taken into account, the most obvious rea- son for teenagers (typically ages thirteen to eighteen, but be- haviors can start as young as the age of ten) wanting to push our buttons is for rebellion. Most teenagers are what you would call "rebels without a cause." Sure, some teens see true injustices and rebel against them, but most simply want to re- bel against us. When you really think about it, it's not unlike two-year-olds; they are once again pushing bound- aries to see how far it can go.

The real reason why kids get on people's nerves? It really depends on the person in question. Some people simply don't like children; others may not like smaller children or older children. Some people are triggered by bad behavior or were raised very strictly. That makes it difficult to deal with rebellious children or little kids trying to push their buttons.

WHAT CAN YOU DO WHEN YOU KNOW THAT YOUR BUTTONS HAVE BEEN PUSHED?

Much like with triggers, you need to first recognize what is it exactly that pushes you over the edge or annoys you about your kids. Is it teenage rebellion? Is it the way they do something? Could it stem from something deeper?

The best thing you can do when you feel as though you may explode, or as though you are about to say something that you don't mean, is to simply walk away. Your kids may not understand it at that moment, but once you've calmed down and you've thought about what exactly frustrated you at that moment, you can go back to them and talk about it.

Your child will likely also be upset at that moment, and so, by walking away for a moment, you're also giving them a chance to calm down. Calmer minds will be clearer minds. It's good to really think about the situation at hand. Are you simply the one being annoyed? Or is your child the one deliberately pushing your buttons? This will help you in focusing your energy on the correct emotion. For example, compassion instead of anger. Focus on yourself for a moment, kids are bound to get up to all kinds of no-good, but our reactions always need to be measured.

Once you start taking a calmer and more supportive stance on things, your child may be the one who realizes that they're wrong. We are their examples, and if we can handle most situations with grace, they will likely have that ability too. You can always use any experience as a lesson. Learn from your mistakes (and their mistakes), and be better every next time.

HOW TO COMMUNICATE YOUR TRIGGERS WITH YOUR CHILD

Communicating with your children is just as important; you need to let them know that certain things are absolutely not okay. It may feel hard to do for some, especially when you're not really much of a communicator. But this is your flesh and blood that we're talking about.

Be sure to take as many deep breaths as you need before the talk. Once you're ready, sit your child down, and explain to them that certain things make you very upset. Explain to them that you understand their reasoning, whatever that may be, in your unique situation, but that it's crucial for you to work together in order to have a safe, calm, and loving home.

When you take a soft approach, they are more likely to understand. It's also important to explain to them that certain things will have certain consequences, especially since they have been clearly communicated. You can even create a list of things that are an absolute no go and put it somewhere. In return, it's also an excellent idea to let your child tell you about what genuinely upsets them too. Try to understand what they say from their perspective and see if a compromise cannot be reached. While our feelings are important because how we feel plays a big role in our manner of parenting, their feelings are just as important. Validating how they feel will help them navigate their feel- ings more easily, especially throughout adulthood.

PARENTAL FREAKOUTS

Now, while we want this calm and serene environment, we may be tempted once again to bottle up our emotions in order to protect our children (Kryza, 2017). But that leads to other issues, making it a vicious circle. Therefore, communi- cating your feelings and worries is essential.

Now, sometimes our kids will still push those buttons because they are, well, kids. And in those situations, it will be important to remember that you are the adult and that you need to react appropriately. These parental freakouts happen, especially when we have clearly communicated our concerns and triggers, and they are ignored.

Being firm is good, but it may still happen, and that in itself may become a trigger. The most important thing to remember is that freaking out sometimes does not make you a bad parent. It also does not mean that you are weak; it's like a trap that we all step in from time to time. But it doesn't have to define you.

These freakouts may also occur when you feel as though your efforts are not appreciated. For example, once your conversation has taken place, and you truly bring the effort to the table, but your child seems to be rebelling all the way. This will inevitably lead to frustration, which, as we know, can easily lead to blowing your top.

How And Why to Avoid These Freak Outs

The most important thing that you can remember is to avoid letting situations escalate. You are the parent, and it's your job to remain in control of your emotions since children are not always able to. Yes, freakouts happen, but we should not let them become the norm.

It's good to ensure that you practice your breathing and other techniques for keeping calm. Kids may sometimes say terrible things that they do not mean, such as "I hate you" while that kind of behavior is not acceptable at all, you need to remember that if you do not retaliate, the situation will likely not escalate any further than that.

It's also good to try and avoid what you believe may cause these. For example, if you know that your child gets moody when you switch the television off, it might be good to avoid the situation by limiting screen time even further. If you have a partner, it may also be a good idea to ask them to take care of that situation for you.

Don't feel bad about it either; you're a team for a reason. While it's good to deal with most situations together, it is okay to ask your partner to step up when you fall short. Avoiding situations that may be too difficult for you is a good step because limiting these freakouts will be better for your kids.

You can also practice anger strategies of your own while roping your kids in. For example, you can create an anger routine that consists of counting, breathing, and perhaps a little rhyme. You can jump in with this as soon as you notice that either you or your kids become angry.

Your little rhyme can be kind of like a mantra.

"Anger is bad; we need to control the emotions we have. I love my parents, and they love me back. That's why we take deep breaths and count to ten. We'll talk when we're calmer, only then."

I've found this method to be helpful for younger children. For older kids, something similar might help, but a more mature mantra might be better.

Children who are often victims of parental freakouts tend to suffer from feelings of guilt and loneliness. They will obviously feel upset, and they may even feel unloved. They don't understand our adult feelings. Again, communication is key (as you'll read in chapter ten); however, even when we explain things to them as best we can, they may still not understand. Especially smaller kids. Children may mistake your frustration for hostility, and that is one thing that we don't want.

CUT YOURSELF SOME SLACK

Parenting is hard; there is no question about that. In the end, I could give you a whole book's worth of advice, you could read through every parenting book and article, but nothing truly prepares you for the reality. You and your kids are unique, and your situation is unique.

Advice is helpful, but you need to also create your own variants of these pieces of advice. As long as you do the best that you can, you will make it through. Be prepared with all the knowledge that you can find, but be willing to do things slightly differently and bend them to the individual needs of your family. Don't get upset when things don't go exactly as planned.

And give yourself a pat on the back, for goodness sakes! You're doing well, and you have the ability to succeed. You're enough! No parent is perfect; we all mess up a million times before we get it right, but that is okay! As long as you are actively working towards being a better version of yourself.

IT TAKES A VILLAGE

Every parent needs a support system; your partner, family, and friends are all important parts of your parenting journey. You don't have to go through this alone. You are not alone. We need a support system in order for us to function and to get the necessary rest and breaks!

Building your support system is essential; you need to make sure that your friends are people that you can trust and people who have your back when you need it. It's also a good idea to ensure that you have a good relationship with your parents and in-laws.

GETTING AWAY FROM YOUR KIDS

You're not a bad parent for wanting a little time to yourself. And it doesn't mean that you don't love your kids. Getting away for a bit is okay, and your support system is important in this regard. I'm not saying that you need to go out every weekend, but at least once every two weeks or so will do you well. Having grandparents who can help take care of the kids every now and again is a great idea. Paid help is another option.

In reality, you can also make a little time for yourself when your kids are home! It's not always possible to get a reliable sitter when you need a break to focus on yourself and your mental health. Therefore, you need to be able to take those few minutes for yourself, even when the kids are around, especially when the overwhelming feelings of parenting start getting to you.

To do this, you can entertain them with activities that are safe and enjoyable, or, if the situation is truly dire and you need a few minutes to collect yourself, it should be okay to make a screen time exception.

That is not a good thing at all and should not become the norm. However, letting them have a few minutes so that you can have a few minutes when you're about to blow your top is okay unless arguments over screen time are a trigger for you.

You know, many bad parental freakouts are triggered by tantrums. These are hard to navigate. But not impossible.

Chapter 6:
TROUBLE WITH TANTRUMS

That was today's parenting tip; It's is all in good fun, but there is actually a little more to it than that!

When my daughter was in preschool, she was a menace with tantrums. I used to struggle with managing my anger, especially around her. But one day, she really threw me over the edge when she pulled a tantrum right around Christmas time. I was working major overtime to afford Christmas, running around doing preparations, and I just lost it. Looking back now, I realize she probably just wanted some attention, and she likely had many feelings of her own that she didn't know how to deal with, just like with most bad behaviors that little ones often resort to.

I want to teach you all about tantrums and what causes them, as well as how to stop them when they start. When we know what causes them, we'll be more likely to know how to deal with them or even stop them!

WHY YOUR KIDS THROW TANTRUMS

Anytime our kids freak out; we call those episodes a tantrum. In reality, there is actually a difference between a meltdown and a tantrum; there are also different kinds of tantrums. When you understand the differences, it's easier to know how to respond.

Tantrums are common amongst children, and they're usually short-lived. They can easily stop when the child is ignored (which we'll get into in a bit) or if they get distracted by something else. I've often found myself laughing at tantrums, one moment, the little darling is throwing a tantrum, and the next moment they're like, "Ooh, a doll." These are not really that serious, but that does not make them any less frustrating.

Meltdowns, however, are serious. These episodes are difficult to control and get through. With a total meltdown, the child is often unable to calm themselves down and won't be easily distracted. The episode may not even stop when we try to comfort them; they may continue until the child has been completely tired out.

The level of severity for normal tantrums ranges from mild and easily distracted to more severe. However, even severe tantrums are not as rough as total meltdowns. These episodes may last throughout their lives and often require further medical assistance. There are also different kinds of meltdowns that may be a result of different underlying causes.

Underlying causes may include ADHD, Attention Deficit Hyperactivity Disorder, anxiety disorders, depression, or even Autism. I've met people who simply don't believe that these things can affect children in such a harsh way, but let me tell you; it can. Acting quickly and getting the help that your little one needs are your best bet.

Just like adults, kids can have anger management issues and a whole range of other problems as well. Of course, we can limit this by keeping ourselves in check, but some level of anger and/or anxiety is inevitable. These are common trig- gers for tantrums.

Two types of tantrums that are most common in children are manipulative tantrums and temper tantrums. Children of the ages one to three also throw tantrums when they simply feel overwhelmed or when they are hungry, scared, or even tired. These little ones don't have the ability to tell us exactly what they need yet, and therefore, they react with tantrums, often because of feeling frustrated that we don't understand what they need or want. We may also be setting expectations that they can't exactly meet, leading to even more frustration.

Here are some other types of tantrums.

- Frustration tantrums are common; sometimes, they get so frustrated that they cry, even when they're too tired to function. This relates most to the above-mentioned.
- Demanding tantrums are what the name suggests. They clearly demand something.
- Refusal tantrums are tantrums that are thrown when they don't want to do something. Again, they can usually clearly let you know what it is that they do not want to do here.

Now, for children ages three to six, the reasoning behind tantrums is a little different. Sure, they may also feel these things, but they are old enough to lean towards either manipulative tantrums or temper tantrums. If this is not handled from a young age, they may last throughout their lives. This would undoubtedly cause damage to their quality of life and may cause further issues into adulthood.

Manipulative tantrums are a child's way of getting what they want. Regardless of what exactly that may be. A simple scenario: You're in a store, and you pass the toy aisle. Your little one asks for a toy, and you say no. Now, the child in question is older than five; therefore, they know exactly what no means, and they know how to push your buttons in order to get you to give in. They know that to keep them quiet, you may give in and get them the toy.

What does said child do? Start screaming. Tantrums are present in different ways, and every child is different, but one common aspect of most tantrums is the hellish scream- ing. You quickly try to get the child to be quiet but to no avail. Therefore, you give in and grab the toy.

The outcome? The child happily goes on with their day, and you are embarrassed, frustrated, and angry. And what's more, you gave in. Therefore, this kind of tantrum is likely to happen again.

It's not just for toys or physical things at all. Children may throw tantrums to manipulate you into doing things or going places. Anything that they can manipulate you with by screaming that's a manipulative tantrum. In a way, you could probably say that other kinds of tantrums may classify as manipulative as well when you think about it.

Temper tantrums are usually related to anger or even frustration, but instead of dealing with the frustration in one way, they resort to a full-blown temper tantrum. Signs of temper tantrums include the infamous 'shriek,' crying, kick- ing, holding their breath, or even other signs of anger that may be more serious such as hurting themselves or other people.

PREVENTING TANTRUMS

It's been said a million times throughout history, in the end, prevention is better than cure! If you can prevent tantrums before they happen, you won't need to worry about the consequences so much or need to worry about what the heck you're supposed to do when your little human freaks out.

Tantrums, meltdowns, whatever you would like to call them, or whatever they mean, are frustrating and sometimes even heartbreaking for parents. Not to mention embarrassing in public. Therefore, if we can stop them before they happen, we can definitely prevent possible parental freakouts as well.

Some parents are so terrified of tantrums that they hardly ever leave the house. Some even tread carefully around their children in order not to upset them, basically giving them free rein. That's obviously not what we're going for. However, there are methods of preventing tantrums that do give your kids a little more control. You might not understand why your three-year-old is throwing a tantrum because they don't like their outfit, but from their perspective, they might simply be frustrated. Imagine having someone do everything for you, to the point where you cannot even choose what to wear. It's not practical to say that you'll always let your toddler choose their own clothes, but you could give them choices (Mlyniec & Harris, 2020).

For example, instead of telling them what they will wear today, grab two or three options of appropriate clothing and ask them which they like best. Giving them options will make them feel as though they have a little more control over themselves. You'll be surprised at what a long way it goes!

This method could be used for a wide variety of things, even for meal times! Okay, again, letting your toddler pick all their meals is not practical. However, you can try giving them one or two options to choose from. "Would you like green beans or sweet potatoes today?" (Mlyniec & Harris, 2020). Some parents do not have the time for this kind of strategy, and that's okay too. But if you have the time before cooking, give it a try!

While we're on the topic of food, it's good to also remember that children have faster metabolisms than we do. They will be hungry again sooner than you will, even after a meal. In order to prevent tantrums as a result of hunger, plan ahead and ensure that you have healthy snacks on hand. Even when you're just going to the grocery store, packing an apple or two will be helpful.

When you're at home, you can keep pre-made snacks in the fridge, such as carrot sticks or even sliced cucumbers. This will help them stay calm until you've finished cooking or until the next meal time arrives. Don't get me wrong, this doesn't mean that you just keep feeding them to keep them busy, but a healthy snack routine is a good idea.

For example, it has been said that children should have at least one or two snacks between meals. Therefore, you could perhaps structure a meal plan for a day as follows.

- Breakfast Cereal/ scrambled eggs and toast/ fruit salad
- Snack Apple/ banana/ crackers
- Lunch Toasted chicken mayo/ tuna
- Snack Carrot sticks/ cheese cubes/ sliced cucumber
- Dinner Lasagna and a salad/ roasted beef and cooked vegetables
- Snack Glass of milk/ hand full of nuts/ mango slices

This is a simple example of a meal plan; you could obviously change it to suit your cooking style and/or time schedule or preferences. When it comes to the evening snack, it might be good to avoid sugary fruits or juices/teas before bed. If you do want to give them a fruit such as mango, be sure to keep it a few hours before bed, as sugary foods may keep them from their sleep.

With this in mind, routine is definitely a recipe for keeping tantrums at bay. Children need routine, and sudden changes may upset them and trigger a tantrum. Therefore, keeping to your routine may prevent these tantrums. It also helps to let them know about any changes that may need to occur early enough.

For example, if you are planning on visiting their grandparents for a weekend, or even an afternoon, it's good to let them know ahead. Try getting them excited about it by reminding them of it for weeks. "We're going to see your Grandparents next weekend! Isn't that exciting?" This can be used for any changes, such as a doctor's visit or if one parent needs to go out of town for a few days.

The next tip is to let them bring their favorite toys to places; I know it's annoying and messy. I know! But letting them keep a toy or two when you go out will be okay. You can still set rules about how many toys they take. But this is another opportunity to give them a choice. You can give them options and ask them which one they would like to bring. We might not understand it as adults, but a stuffed toy, a truck, or even a blanket may be the source of the little one's comfort.

That's completely normal too, while as parents, we like to think that we are their comfort, and we are, as you know. But we are not their only source of comfort. And as they grow older, they'll find comfort in many other things. That's normal, too; obviously, we need to look out for what they find comfort in since children can develop bad habits just like we can. Be careful not to let food become a form of comfort, for example. This could lead to eating disorders such as BED (Binge Eating Disorder) which is characterized by overeating and using food as comfort during bouts of depression and/or happiness.

WHAT TO DO DURING A TANTRUM/ HOW TO STOP THEM FASTER

The most important thing you can do is to remain calm and in control of your own emotions. Yes, I know that it's diffi- cult. Especially when you have anger management issues yourself, but it's crucial to demonstrate that you will not tolerate this kind of behavior by not falling into the very same trap.

Some people have mentioned that ignoring a tantrum is a good option. I feel that it's definitely an option but assess the situation first. Temper tantrums should be dealt with firmly; otherwise, they may get out of control. Total meltdowns need to be dealt with differently as well because they can also get out of control very quickly.

If you're in the middle of a total meltdown or temper tantrum, it's good to get your child out of the public eye. Not just to save you from embarrassment, but to ensure that they do not hurt themselves or anyone else.

You can try distracting them with something else for milder tantrums. But for these out-of-control wild rides, I find it a good idea to hold them and try to comfort them. Yes, you need to be firm. However, at that moment, they need to be reassured. Once your child has calmed down, you can give them a stern talking to and discuss the consequences for their actions. Never discipline a child when they are actively in the middle of a meltdown or temper tantrum; it will likely just make the situation worse. You should also never engage in these tantrums when you are extremely upset either because this may lead to yelling and further angry parenting.

For severe freakouts like the above-mentioned, your best bet may be to have a special and safe space where you can place your child to calm down. For example, some people feel that grabbing an out-of-control child and simply holding them tightly until they calm down is helpful. I wouldn't say it's bad, but I fear that it may add to frustration in severe cases.

Letting them cool down in a safe space may be your best option. I'm definitely not saying that you should lock them in their room all alone; this may actually cause intense feelings that they may not be able to handle. Feelings of abandonment are common in these cases.

For this reason, I believe that it's a good idea to stay with them. Even when it's difficult, if you have a partner, it may be helpful to take turns, especially when you are feeling frustrated as well. Stay with them for as long as you can, and then tag your partner in so that you can have a few minutes to cool down.

The worst thing that you can ever do is to give in to what- ever they may be demanding if that is the situation. As I explained during the little scenario, giving in and just letting them have what they were throwing a tantrum for will inevitably cause a repeat cycle. They're smarter than we think, these little buggers. They'll quickly realize that this is how they get what they want.

Acknowledge their emotions, and let them know that they are heard. But that they need to learn to express their feel- ings in the right way and that you're here to help them do that.

Do you know what I read one day? And it completely made sense to me. In an article written by Lauren Tamm (a very helpful writer, look her up!) on a website called "The military wife and mom," I read that you need to match the intensity of your child. Acknowledge their feelings, yes, but perhaps instead of speaking in a calm voice, speak as though you know and truly understand their frustration. That way, they'll feel heard and understood. For example, instead of saying, "I understand that you're angry because of XYZ," try going, "You're so ANGRY because you WANT XZY, how FRUSTRATING!

But, we need to do the following". It doesn't mean yell at them; it means that you can try demon- strating their frustration back towards them, as though you really understand what they're going through (even if you don't, I mean, I wouldn't cry over a stuffed animal but to each their own).

Don't ever take the things that they may spit at you during an episode personally. They often don't mean the things they say when they're so upset, just like adults. You should also try not to feel bad about yourself. You're not a bad parent! Kids throw tantrums; you're not the only one who has to deal with it!

If you were, there would not be so much helpful advice on the topic out there because nobody would have taken the time to conduct the proper research. But it affects millions of parents and children all over the world. Regardless of culture, country, religion, or anything else, it happens.

According to experts, it's also not a good idea to respond sarcastically or to try and tell them how they need to feel. For example, telling a six-year-old that they're too big to be throwing a tantrum over a lost toy is not a good thing. Whether they are too old or not, they are still actively experi- encing these feelings. When it comes to sarcasm, it's easy to say things such as, "Oh, you want juice now? I want a brand new bike, but you don't see that happening right now" (Miller, 2018). But it doesn't help the situation, and in fact, it makes the child feel further invalidated.

All in all, the best way to stop a tantrum, or a temper tantrum, is to stop your own.

Chapter 7:
HOW TO TAME YOUR BEAST

Let's focus on how to manage and prevent your anger for the benefit of your children.

DIFFERENT WAYS TO MANAGE AND PREVENT ANGER

Let's start by listing different ways in which you can manage and/or prevent your anger by taking care of yourself and your body and, more importantly, your mind!

- Worthy of mentioning multiple times, until the fact sinks in, self-care. This is your number one defense against your anger. Ensuring that you are taken care of is important for the good of your family, and of course, for your own good.
- We've briefly touched on the topic of sleep and why it's important, but getting enough sleep is not always that easy. Discussing how to get the proper amount of sleep will benefit you.
- Meditation is thousands of years old, and it is practiced all over the world. Sometimes for religious purposes,

other times for the purpose of peacefulness.

- Mindfulness relates to meditation in many ways, and we'll take a deeper look at how it can help you either paired with meditation or on its own.
- Exercise is crucial for your health, physically and mentally. It can also be a fun activity for the family! Alone time is also a great defense against anger and frustration. Sometimes you might even need alone time in the form of being away from your partner as well. I know that I said that everyone tells us about this, but the fact is that it really does help. As mentioned before, if you are able to get your alone time, take it. Calming down before reacting to a situation will help you think clearly. It will enhance your problem-solving skills when you have a clear mind.
- Distractions come in handy for many things, and when used the right way, they may also help you relieve your anger and/or frustration.
- Try getting an anger buddy! This may sound a little silly to some, but I've found it highly effective! When you feel as though you're about to explode, dial-up your anger buddy! This can be someone who has the same issues as you do, and you can also help them when they feel as though they may explode. It comes down to support. You need the support of like- minded people or of the people you love.

- Keeping a journal may also help. For example, practice leaving the situation that has angered you and going to your room. You can write all the angry thoughts that you have down, every nasty word that you wish to say to the person that your anger is targeted at, and even the things you want to do, like throw a plate. When you've calmed down, read through what you've written. I've found that reading through this anger after the incident will often leave you relieved. Relieved that you did not do or say any of those things. It also puts the situation into perspective. Once the journal is full, burn it. Kind of like cleansing the soul of all the anger. Some people enjoy burning the pages as soon as they have calmed down.

Now that we've mentioned a few different things let's take a deeper look at four of the most important ones.

SELF- CARE

Self-care is a way not to simply manage your anger but to totally take control of it. It's not binge eating or drinking the way popular television shows would have us believe. It relates to things that promote health, both physically and mentally. Anything that can be destructive or lead to nega- tive side effects will not be classified as self-care.

Now, let's get one thing straight, self-care is not solely for women or for mothers at all. It's for all human beings; as men, we need to take care of ourselves too. I find it difficult to believe that the world frowns on men who want to take care of themselves. This circles back to our mental health as well.

The world is so afraid of men being portrayed as 'feminine' that they forget that as human beings, we deserve to be taken care of as well. In a nutshell, yes, you can take regular showers, use lotions, and focus on your mental health just as much as anyone else. When you are taken care of, you focus more on your emotions, which means that finding the root of your anger is easier and more practical.

Self-care is avoiding bad habits and embracing good ones. Let's look at different things that you can do in order to practice self-care regularly or even daily!

The very first tip is probably the most simple one. However, many people don't really realize how it benefits you. Taking a bath or a shower is such a pleasant part of self-care; some people even take them twice a day!

A nice, hot shower or bath actually has a great physical and mental effect. You see, your muscles relax when you are warm. The fact that a bath or shower is usually taken alone (hopefully, if you have a partner to help with the kids for a while) also adds to the calming effect.

Therefore, it not only helps you manage your anger, but it helps you manage stress by calming you down. I've met people who jump in the shower multiple times a day just to calm down. I suppose that it's not really a practical method, but if it works for you and your anger/ anxiety/ stress is severe, then to each their own!

Now, I know that skincare is frowned upon by men; again, toxic masculinity is likely our main reason. But it's actually important, and it has been said to help reduce symptoms of anger and other issues.

I suppose a skincare routine will not calm you down in the moment, but it's one of those things that will help you in the long run. For the moms out there, I am very sure that you understand exactly what I mean!

I've often been told by women that there is nothing quite as relaxing as taking a hot shower and then sitting down and spoiling yourself with skincare products. It makes them feel clean, shiny, and new! It also boosts self-confidence, which is a huge plus.

Men may be more reluctant, and I get that. But it's worth a shot! Couples who engage in skincare routines together also often testify that it's a great bonding experience. It's a few minutes away from the daily stressors where you and your partner can simply enjoy taking care of yourselves and of each other. Let's face it; most women would be over the moon about getting to apply that face mask for you anyway. What do you have to lose?

A very underestimated form of self-care is the simple act of reading a book. While you're taking the time to limit screen time in the home, you might also want to try adding a reading hour to your daily routine! You can get the whole family in on it (if your kids are old enough to read by them- selves). You don't have to involve everyone; some people prefer quiet reading time by themselves.

Reading stimulates your mind, and it's a great way to relax. I've also found that reading before bed makes it easier to fall asleep! But it's not just that; reading together as a family can be a great bonding experience as well.

One of my favorite acts of self-care is listening to music. There's something about the way the music speaks to the soul. Musicians often describe playing their instruments as the most calming and magical experience. They often use it as a defense against anger, frustration, stress, and more!

Not all of us have this talent, but for those of us who don't, listening to music is still a great way to relax. Apparently, music is also great for your brain, so that's something else to consider!

Self-care is also eating right! I know it's the most tempting thing in the world for some of us. There's nothing quite like eating a slice of cake after a long day. But you know what? That one slice of cake isn't the end-all. It becomes a problem when that slice of cake is daily. Eating enough of the right foods will help you feel more energetic, which helps in preventing anger issues that stem from exhaustion.

GETTING A GOOD NIGHT' S SLEEP

There are different things that you can do in order to ensure enough sleep. But for some people, these things may not be as effective as they would like. Insomnia is a real problem for some people, and obviously, insomnia plus anger management issues will equal disaster.

I'm going to list a few things that you can do to help your sleep schedule. However, if these simple home techniques do not work, I would urge you once more to seek the counsel of a healthcare professional. Not getting enough sleep is obviously not good for your physical health either. In fact, not sleeping enough over many years may lead to a higher risk of heart disease and other issues (CDC, 2021).

Caffeine is probably the most common thing that people tell you to cut down on for better sleep. I have to agree with the fact that caffeine elevates your heart rate, and of course, it has a waking effect. Some people are more caffeine sensitive than others; therefore, they may be more likely to be kept awake from one cup of coffee, whereas someone else may not be that affected.

What you may not know is that since caffeine elevates your heart rate, it can also worsen symptoms of anger management issues. This is because slowing your heart rate down and remaining calm is your goal, right? Coffee undoes that. Some people may even have health anxiety, in which case their elevated pulse may lead to anxiety as well.

In the end, I would say that avoiding caffeine (which includes soda, chocolates, and other things that may contain caffeine) after around 4 pm is probably your best bet. Whether you are caffeine sensitive or not, it does affect your body. While you may not notice it while you're actively having a lot of coffee, you'll definitely notice the difference when you've started cutting down.

I've previously mentioned that limiting screen time before bed and reading before bed will also help you. Therefore, I will not dive deeply into that now, but keep it in mind!

It's good to work around your schedule in order to ensure that you're getting enough sleep. I know exactly how tough this can be. Especially when you're working long hours and the kids are keeping you busy for the rest of the time! However, it's definitely worth trying to work around.

For example, if you have a partner, you could take turns sleeping in/going to bed early. Let's say that you are going to bed early tonight, and your partner is staying up to handle the kids. Tomorrow, you will be the one who gets up earlier for the children so that your partner may sleep in a little.

Ideally, you could force yourself to go to bed at around 8 pm, which means that even if it takes you a whole hour to fall asleep, you'll still have had over eight hours of sleep by 6 am! This way, you get a good night's rest, and you get up early and get the kids ready for school/keep them busy so that your partner may sleep in a little.

The next evening, you can change it up, and you will be able to sleep in a while your partner goes to bed early. This way, you both get enough sleep, at least every second night, and even then, the extra hour or so in the mornings will still really help!

It's also not a bad idea to take a short nap during the day if you can manage it. When it comes to naps, never take them after mid-day; this might keep you up at night, even if you do manage the time to get to bed a little earlier. Naps should also not be longer than about an hour.

Now, experts might tell you that naps should be shorter, but for me, I definitely can't fall asleep within a few minutes. If you are one of those people who can, that's great! You should limit your nap to 20 minutes in total. But if you're like me, then you can definitely stretch it to an hour to make up for the time it takes to fall asleep.

On that note, people who suffer from insomnia may have even more trouble falling asleep. It may be tempting to try and nap during the day if you have severe trouble with sleep- ing; however, experts agree that napping during the day is not good for people who have trouble with sleeping (Mayo Clinic Staff, 2020). See, as a parent, your issue may not be with falling asleep at all, and in this case, as mentioned above, a short nap should be okay.

But when you have insomnia, you really need to focus on being able to sleep during the evening in order to get your rest because even a short day nap may make it even harder to fall asleep later on. It's a difficult situation because we need sleep, and it makes sense that if you cannot sleep during the evening, you should try and get your sleep in whenever you are actually able to do so. But this is seemingly not the case.

I also need to mention that if you, unfortunately, do smoke cigarettes, it's probably also best to avoid them at least two hours before bed since they are also a stimulant. Which means they may also keep you from your sleep.

Along with the correct medications for treating insomnia, it has also been said that staying active during the day will help you fall asleep. You can use tips mentioned for better sleep for insomnia as well, but the correct medication may be crucial to your health.

MEDITATION AND MINDFULNESS FOR ANGER

Meditation can be guided by a trained instructor, or it can be done in solitude. It depends on your personal situation and how comfortable you are with other people in your space.

Meditation is said to help us better understand and recog- nize our feelings, including anger. This helps us to better calculate how we need to respond instead of responding impulsively (Guided Meditation for Anger, n.d.).

Meditation uses one of a few techniques to better one's ability to achieve a peaceful state of mind and more. It focuses on at- tention and awareness in order to achieve this (Cherry, 2020).

Mindfulness is one of the techniques that can be used for meditation.

Some simple acts of meditation include the following:

- Breath focus (basically focusing on your breathing while tuning everything else out).
- 4-7-8 breathing is a technique that is used by many people all over the world. It's commonly used for anger, anxiety, and more. It's quite easy to do; you'll breathe in for four seconds, hold your breath for seven seconds, and then breathe out for eight seconds. It has been said that this technique also helps people with sleep!
- Progressive muscle relaxation, otherwise known as (PMR) first became known somewhere in the 1930s by a physician named Edmund Jacobson. It's basically tensing and relaxing different muscles in your body. This is a great way to relax yourself, and again, it may even help you sleep better, which will, in turn, will, lead to better anger management.
- Mindfulness is a great technique for meditation; it's as simple as the following:
- Recognize
- Realize
- Breathe
- Body scan (a body scan can be done by closing your

eyes and focusing on every part of your body from tip to toe. Becoming aware of every sensation and part is the goal.)

EXERCISE FOR ANGER MANAGEMENT

Exercise has been used throughout history as a great method of relieving symptoms of stress, and anxiety, among many other mental illnesses. It obviously also links to better physical health.

Exercise is a great way to "blow off steam." Going for a run when you feel like you're about to blow your top will help you calm yourself down. Exercise helps the production and release of endorphins which are responsible for that "good feeling" they are also said to help with pain relief. Endor- phins help relieve stress and frustration and bring a sense of calmness with them. Therefore, I believe that exercise is a great way to relieve anger as well.

Some great exercises that you can try out in order to help you manage your anger are the following:

- Aerobics
- Jogging
- Bike ride

- Boxing
- Jump rope
- Tai Chi
- Yoga

These are also great for your overall health, which ties back to self-care! It's good to find a type of exercise that you personally enjoy. Doing something that you enjoy will help you stay committed to it.

Regularly practicing anger management techniques is great at lowering your chances of outbursts in the long run; however, in the moment, it can still be hard not to get angry.

Sometimes despite your best efforts, it still happens. You find yourself about to boil over. The good thing is that by now if you've applied some of the other methods, you should be able to recognize when this happens. That's already a step in the right direction! Of course, it's easier to stop this if you can notice it before it escalates too much.

Here are some good tips for when you find yourself in the moment and you realize that it may escalate further without action.

- Taking time out to calm down in solitude is just as effective here.

- Do a grounding exercise (I will explain this a little further down).
- Write down your thoughts.
- Blow steam off by spending some time with a punching bag!
- As always, focus on your breathing.

These exercises will definitely help you to stop and recognize your feelings in the moment. It may even prevent you from doing or saying things that you may not mean.

LET' S TALK ABOUT GROUNDING TECHNIQUES

Grounding techniques allow you to pull yourself from the emotions or the current situation. Basically, 'grounding' yourself when you feel as though you may slip and fall or lose control.

The most commonly known grounding technique is the five senses method. This is also commonly used to combat panic attacks. After a few deep breaths, you'll focus on your senses, starting with what you can see.

Recognize five things that you can see around you. Anything at all, curtains, your shoes, another person, anything that you can clearly see.

Next, you'll focus on four things that you are able to feel. It can be the wind blowing softly on your skin or even a book that you can pick up.

For the third step, you'll focus on three things that you are able to hear. In bouts of anger, your own heartbeat might be one of them. But it could also be the birds outside or the rain on your roof.

You'll then focus on two things that you're able to smell. Perhaps your own cologne? Your partner's perfume, cooking, the smell of your leather couches, or anything in between.

And finally, you'll focus on one thing that you can taste. Reach for a healthy snack or even a piece of sugar-free gum, and savor the flavor. See what I did there? Jokes aside, this method has helped countless people ground themselves in order to calm down.

Keeping your feelings in check is important, but a good way to heal and prevent anger in the future is to communicate effectively. Many issues can be avoided with the help of effective communication.

Chapter 8:
COMMUNICATION IS KEY

Communication is a way of expressing yourself verbally. It's critical for all relationships in life, including your relationship with your children, partner, colleagues, and friends. Communicating clearly is essential for parenting and relationships. Nobody knows what truly goes on in your mind. Not letting people know how you feel or what your boundaries are can lead to situations that may escalate your anger management issues and/or other mental health-related issues.

It's easy to misunderstand someone or to have someone misunderstand us. Misunderstandings probably create 90% of preventable escalations. Remember how little ones cannot properly communicate their needs yet? This obviously leads to tantrums and us becoming frustrated and angry.

You know what? The same issue may exist well into adulthood if communication is not clear enough. Some people find it difficult to communicate their needs with others for most of their lives. This can cause depression and other related issues. Many people then turn inward in order to protect themselves from the world that seemingly just does not understand them. While this is possible, communication may be the true culprit. It's unlikely that nobody will under- stand you. Regardless of what your interests are or what kind of person you are, there are a lot of people in the world. Chances are, someone will be able to relate with you.

Communication is not always verbal; body language also plays a role in communication. It's important to look out for signs of body language that may indicate that someone is feeling different from what they may be saying, especially with your own children. They may be throwing a tantrum over a toy that they want, but they are rubbing their eyes and yawning. This is a clear indication that your child is actually just exhausted, but they may be fighting the exhaustion, or they don't know how to properly communicate with you. Smaller children may not even fully understand that they are actually just tired; all they know is that they don't feel well, and they don't understand why.

Other common body language signs to look out for are:

Clenching fists may indicate anger. Things like a furrowed brow or tightened lips may also indicate anger. It's important to look out for these signs in your children because you can help them deal with their anger if you recognize it. It's also important to look out for these signs in other people so that you can prepare yourself for what may come. Recognizing anger before it explodes may also help you to help someone else. Or even to realize when you've said or done something that may not be entirely right and/or acceptable. There is always room for improvement!

Pulling away from you or from another adult. This is actually very important; if your child shows signs of being uncom- fortable with an adult, you need to take that seriously. They may say hello, or act as though they are okay with a hug, but their body language will speak for them. A child who is uncomfortable around an adult may have been through a traumatic experience regarding that adult or another adult. I know that we don't want to talk about it, but it needs to be said. You cannot blindly trust anyone with your children, even family or friends.

This is where communication is also crucial; you need to be able to communicate with your child regarding why they feel the way they do. This is so that you can assess the situation and recognize if any form of abuse may have taken place. If there is no open communication between you and your child, this will be difficult.

A child who seems to pull away from you may have also been through a traumatic experience with another adult. Or they may simply not be comfortable with physical affection; that's okay too. What is not okay is forcing a child to hug you or anyone else if they are not comfortable with it. This is their first lesson in boundaries. I've read countless articles on this recently. It's apparently vital for us to recognize and respect the boundaries that our children set in order to teach them the skills they need to set boundaries in their later years.

You know how we're always telling our children not to slouch? Or at least, our parents were always telling us not to slouch. Well, it turns out that this may be due to low self-esteem. Someone who is proud and happy might more commonly walk tall, while someone who does not feel that confident may not. It's important to look out for this in your own children. Self-esteem issues may become severe, and they may impact the rest of their lives.

WHY COMMUNICATION IS IMPORTANT FOR PARENTS WITH ANGER ISSUES

It's important to effectively communicate with one's child if one struggles with anger management issues, any other issues related to anger, or even other mental health-related issues. Your children need to understand your feelings, and they need to understand that you still love them. Even when you're frustrated or angry, they also need to understand that how you feel is not necessarily their fault. Effectively communicating with your children may also prevent build-ups of rage that may negatively affect you, your family, and your quality of life.

The big issue with communication is that we learn how to communicate in our formative years. That means that if we had a difficult upbringing, our communication skills might not be up to standard. For example, let's say that you had angry parents as well. You learned how to communicate from your parents, and you took notice of how they commu- nicated with each other.

Now that you're an adult, your communication style may not be appropriate for your situation, especially when you have children of your own. How they learn to communicate will also depend on their situation and upbringing. You're not only responsible for your own communication but for theirs as well.

I know, it's a lot of pressure. Parenting is a lot of pressure. We're responsible for these whole little human beings who will be adults, parents, and partners one day as well. I suppose that once again, it ties back to the cycle that needs to be broken.

HOW TO COMMUNICATE THROUGH ESCAL ATED CONFLICTS

Your number one communication skill during active conflicts is active listening. Active listening is genuinely quieting down and paying attention to what the other person is saying. In order to engage in active listening, you need to be sure that they have your attention for that moment. Even when you feel as though you are the angry one, you can take your breaths, ground yourself, and then tell them that you are ready to listen.

It's okay to ask for a few minutes before listening; older children will understand this, and letting them have a few minutes to calm down and think before they speak will also help. Younger children may not be so understanding; in fact, they may also be hard to understand. But you can still try active listening and putting yourself in their shoes.

Listening to what your child or anyone else has to say does not mean that you need to comply with their demands, regardless of their reasoning. It simply means that you need to give them your attention and let them know that their opinions and feelings are valid. Even if they are four years old and they feel as though they deserve a second ice cream.

Now, the next tip that I think is very important is being assertive. It's okay to be assertive when it comes to serious conflicts. However, there is a fine line between being assertive and being rude and/or angry.

Assertive communication is clear and to the point. "You are

not having another ice cream today. But we can revisit the situation in a few days", "You are not going out tonight," or even "I feel that my workload is full at the moment, I cannot take on this new task."

So, it is okay and important to express your concerns as well, and you may be assertive, but be careful not to come off as 'mean,' as our little ones would say! It's all about how you say what you feel. You know, you can even say something negative about someone in a way that is less offensive and more constructive.

For example, let's say that your teenager dresses inappropriately, whatever that may mean to you, personally. You can let them know about this in the following way.

"You are such an intelligent and brilliantly pleasant person; however, the way you dress makes you seem XYZ. It's important to be able to express yourself, and I support you in being the truest version of yourself that you can be. But you are a little young for XYZ at this time; I understand that you may be tempted to dress this way because of XYZ; however, XYZ is an issue right now."

I know that this may not be the best example, but there are other things that can relate to this as well. Let's say that your partner has a bit of a drinking problem.

"You know that I love you and that I care for you; therefore, I would like to spend many more years with you. The children would like this as well. Alcohol is not good for your health, and as parents, we also need to set good examples for our children. I know this is hard for you, but I am here to support you in any way that I can."

The point of this kind of communication is the fact that it is to the point, but it is still polite and understanding.

HOW TO COMMUNICATE WITH YOUR CHILD

It's important to regularly communicate with your child in order to strengthen your bond and in order to encourage good communication skills. It also helps to know what is going on in their lives to be able to assess whether you may need to step in and help them.

I know it's hard to hear some of the things going on in the lives of our children, especially teenagers who may be becoming curious about all kinds of things. But it's impor- tant to listen without judgment and to offer support and assistance where it is needed.

Our children need to know that they can talk to us about anything. Whether it's about the friend who bit them today at recess or about experimenting with things that they should probably not be experimenting with. If we flip out over everything, they will likely not come to us the next time that they have an issue.

I don't need to tell you what kids can get up to, especially teenagers. I am sure that you know. If they feel safe enough to talk to us, then at least we can help them with the matter. If they are too afraid to talk to us, they may find themselves in terrible situations or even dangerous ones.

Communicating regularly helps you develop a healthy relationship; it helps your child be more open about their feelings as well. It also helps you both solve any possible issues faster when you can both communicate your needs clearly to the other.

Here are some ways in which you can begin to communicate with your child:

- Let them speak; even when you are feeling frustrated or angry, give them a chance to voice their concerns. Don't treat them as though they are inferior, they may be children, but they are still little people.
- Don't be afraid to ask them about how their day was, and be prepared to listen to all kinds of playground nonsense with genuine interest.
- Regularly ask them about how they feel. It can be about

going somewhere, doing something, or even just about how they feel in general.

- Be sure to always make eye contact. When your eyes drift around, it may make them feel as though you are not truly interested in what they are saying. It may also make them feel as though they are not enough to catch your attention. Look at them and practice active listening.
- It may also be a good idea to ensure that when you are talking, you have no other distractions such as your cellphone. You can even let your partner know that you need a moment alone. That's okay!

The fact is, communication is key. For any relationship. But especially for your relationship with your children. The above can also be used when communicating with your part- ner, friends, or family.

Communicating with colleagues is just as important, and you can definitely use the tips above in that regard as well. Just be prepared to be a little more professional but still be assertive about your boundaries and needs.

Teaching your children about effective communication will benefit them in the long run. Luckily, if we teach them the right things from a young age, they won't have to recover or change their communication skills when they are older because they will already be on the right track!

You are capable of changing your communication skills from bordering on rude/ negative to positive and encouraging. You'll see! Remember that keeping your head high and using clear and concise language will also benefit you.

Conclusion

When we talk about anger management, we are talking about how you control your emotional and physiolog- ical responses to situations that cause anger. You cannot avoid these situations, and you cannot avoid becoming angry at times; that is only natural. However, you can learn to control how you react.

LOVE, PEACE, UNDERSTANDING, CHILDREN

You've made it! The patience it took to read through this book in order to better yourself, and the lives of your chil- dren proves that you have the patience to make the change.

You've learned what anger is; you've learned how to control it. You've found the root of your anger and other issues, and you've learned how to heal your own scars for the benefit of you and your family.

The most important part of becoming a better version of your- self is healing from your own trauma. And I hope that my book has at least nudged you in the right direction. True healing will take much longer than we'd like it to, and it will definitely take work. But again, it's worth it, and you are worth it!

You know now that anger affects people differently and that your personality type definitely does play a role. Who knew? I definitely recommend that you and your partner both take the test on 16personalities.com. You never know what else you may learn about your personality type and how it can positively influence the quality of your life.

The one chapter that I really want you to take with you is chapter eight. Communication is key! It will make or break a relationship, and it's all down to you, especially when it comes to younger children who still need to learn valuable communication skills.

On the other hand, you've even learned that technology can play a role! Who knew? Technology is both a gift and a burden. The way we use it will make the difference! It will benefit you to try and limit the use of certain technologies and to encourage outside play and reading. Spending time as a family will also help you bond with your loved ones. Remember, while you're teaching your children that screen time needs to be limited, you also need to limit your own in order to set a good example and to benefit yourself as well. "Do what I say, not what I do" is not an effective method of parenting. It has been proven again and again. Don't fall into that trap! Check yourself too!

The practical tips and information that I have shared will

hopefully carry you to victory. You know what your triggers are and how to deal with them. You've also learned more about tantrums and meltdowns. These tips will help you weather the storms of parenthood because even though we'd like to believe that parenting could be a breeze, it definitely is not always.

Now that you've got the tools to tie down your anger, put them to work! Your goal is right around the corner. You can reach it if you put the work in. Nothing comes easy in life, and the things that we work for the hardest, are the things that are the most valuable.

Change is possible, bit by bit, day by day. Generation by generation.

It all begins with you.

Children and anger, you can do it!

EMILY KENDALL

© Copyright 2021 - All rights reserved.

....

The content contained within this book may not be reproduced, duplicated or transmitted without direct written permission from the author or the publisher.

Under no circumstances will any blame or legal responsibility be held against the publisher, or author, for any damages, reparation, or monetary loss due to the information contained within this book. Either directly or indirectly.

Legal Notice:

This book is copyright protected. This book is only for personal use. You cannot amend, distribute, sell, use, quote or paraphrase any part, or the content within this book, without the consent of the author or publisher.

Disclaimer Notice:

Please note the information contained within this document is for educational and entertainment purposes only. All effort has been executed to present accurate, up to date, and reliable, complete information. No warranties of any kind are declared or implied. Readers acknowledge that the author is not engaging in the rendering of legal, financial, medical or professional advice. The content within this book has been derived from various sources. Please consult a licensed professional before attempting any techniques outlined in this book.

By reading this document, the reader agrees that under no circumstances is the author responsible for any losses, direct or indirect, which are incurred as a result of the use of information contained within this document, including, but not limited to, — errors, omissions, or inaccuracies.

....
Thank you for buying this book.

www.ingramcontent.com/pod-product-compliance
Lightning Source LLC
Chambersburg PA
CBHW030304100526
44590CB00012B/514